PRAISE AWKWARD SPIRITUALITY

"In a world that values big, better, and efficient, Christianity has often adopted the same values and built its systems and metrics up on them. The result: something that looks far different than Jesus. Simple, small, humble, vulnerable, and friendship are not popularly touted concepts in Christian practice, yet they are exactly what the world needs more of, now more than ever. Ryan Taylor's work, words, and decades of engaged practice challenge and encourage us to embody something very different than most of us were taught. He's a humble guide on a path that doesn't lead to a shiny scenic lookout point, but rather down a rocky, beautiful road that changes our lives, our hearts, our communities, our practices forever."

—Kathy Escobar, Co-Pastor of The Refuge and author of *Practicing: Changing Yourself to Change to Change the World* and *Faith Shift: Finding Your Way Forward When Everything You Believe is Coming Apart*

"*Awkward Spirituality* is a doorway into what incarnational ministry looks like when it is at its best. The blessed community that is Network, and the stories that have captured Ryan's life and heart, jump off the page with gut-wrenching trauma and hopeful humor; Christ in every person, story, and interaction. *Awkward Spirituality* is exactly what the world needs—a way of life filled with humility, joy, hopefulness, liberation, and the contemplative way."

—Preston Adams, Regional Director of the Central Area, Denver Area Youth for Christ

"What *Awkward Spirituality* offers is a mystical view that is so urgent at the moment. It ventilates the world with tenderness and puts first things recognizably first. Ryan Taylor helps us see as God sees, and his authentic voice gently guides us to embrace the open-hearted thrill of a God so spacious."

—Father Gregory Boyle, Founder & Director of Homeboy Industries, Author of *Tattoos on the Heart* and *Barking to the Choir*

"In *Awkward Spirituality*, Ryan Taylor shares wisdom from the bottom, the kind born of hardship, brutal honesty, poverty, and suffering. It's the kind of wisdom we need, and what we deeply want, but few have the courage to surrender to it. Taylor is in process of this continual surrender, which is why we need this book and the wisdom he shares."

—Michael Hidalgo, Lead Pastor of Denver Community Church, Author of *Changing Faith: Questions, Doubts and Choices about an Unchanging God*

"I invite you to share in the stories of this book about engaging the divine depths of our everyday lives. Ryan Taylor is a master at storytelling, whether it is his story or someone else's. It is always a blessing to sit with him. You will hear the echoing wisdom of Psalms 42:7, "Deep calls to deep," as you read about Ryan's call in *Awkward Spirituality*. In chapter 3, celebrate the particularity of Ryan's story as he leads you to "the Living sound in the form of a dove's gentle song." In chapter 4, share in the deeper meaning and "authentic hope that results from the possibility and healing bonds of friendship." Open yourself to the practice of listening toward the heart of Reality—the Loving heart of God. Join Ryan in the reality of *kairos* time and being seen by the Great I AM. Again, I invite you to give yourself this gift of engagement. Like me, you will count it a blessing on your list of gratitudes."

—Penny Salazar-Philips, Licensed clinical social worker and former Director of the LIFE Program at Mile High Ministries

AWKWARD

spirituality

the divinity of ordinary life

Ryan C. Taylor

Published in the United States by Kindle Enterprise Publishing.

Scripture quotations are from the Holy Bible, New Living Translation (NLT) copyright © 1996, 2004, 2007, 2013, 2015 by Tyndale House Foundation. Scripture quotations identified KJV are from The King James Version. Scripture quotations identified TLB are from The Living Bible © 1971 by Tyndale House Foundation. Scripture quotations identified ESV are from the English Standard Version copyright © 2001 by Crossway, a publishing ministry of Good News Publishers.

Printed in the United States of America
Cover design and book layout: Emily Dykes / Laura Emily Illustration
Editor: Lauren DiCecio Stevens / Ink Well
First Edition.

Library of Congress Cataloging-in-Publication Data is available.

Trade paper ISBN: 978-1-7923-5374-1

AWKWARD

spirituality

the divinity of ordinary life

Ryan C. Taylor

Published in the United States by Kindle Enterprise Publishing.

Scripture quotations are from the Holy Bible, New Living Translation (NLT) copyright © 1996, 2004, 2007, 2013, 2015 by Tyndale House Foundation. Scripture quotations identified KJV are from The King James Version. Scripture quotations identified TLB are from The Living Bible © 1971 by Tyndale House Foundation. Scripture quotations identified ESV are from the English Standard Version copyright © 2001 by Crossway, a publishing ministry of Good News Publishers.

Printed in the United States of America
Cover design and book layout: Emily Dykes / Laura Emily Illustration
Editor: Lauren DiCecio Stevens / Ink Well
First Edition.

Library of Congress Cataloging-in-Publication Data is available.

Trade paper ISBN: 978-1-7923-5374-1

AWKWARD SPIRITUALITY
THE DIVINITY OF ORDINARY LIFE

By Ryan C. Taylor

Edited by: Lauren DiCecio Stevens / Ink Well
Design by: Emily Dykes / Laura Emily Illustration

For my friend, Angela.

The mysticism of everyday life is the deepest mysticism of all.

—Jürgen Moltmann

CONTENTS

A BEGINNING

"You'd better not be here to fix me!"

Those were the words—wise and timely words—of a fingerless man called Kickback. It was my very first day at Network Coffee House when Kickback looked me dead in the eye and offered that weighty greeting.

Network is a hospitality house for the marginalized street community of downtown Denver, and in hindsight, I can't imagine a better orientation to the beautifully awkward life of chaplaincy, presence, and provocation.

If you're reading this book with me, I'm going to picture you walking right up to me in the same bold manner as Kickback while uttering those same words of welcome and warning.

"You'd better not be here to fix me!"

I hear you. And I assure you this is not a book about fixing.

Within the human species, it's my type—male, specifically white Christian male—who is really into fixing stuff. Historically, we think we know what's best for you . . . and due to that destructive delusion, we're all more than a little worse off.

It's the year 2020 and as I write this, America is smoldering. There's a collective dizziness and exhaustion unlike anything we've ever experienced.

I feel an acute powerlessness.

Breonna Taylor and George Floyd are the latest black lives to be lost at the hands of unhinged police violence. A virus called Covid-19 has its teeth clenched on our nation's physical and mental health. The rhetoric from our country's leadership has produced migraine-like tension and a violent division like we've never seen before.

And I'm powerless to fix it.

So, what is my intention in the following pages?

My sincere desire is to participate in, as well as humbly invite you into, a movement from the frenetic fixing energy of the head toward the attentive, curious, healing energy of the heart.

Awkward Spirituality is a very personal telling of my education, evolution, and humiliation toward developing the heart of a contemplative activist. I'm banking on the idea that the more personal and honest I can be, the more relatable you'll find the book.

I fulfill the roles of director and chaplain of the Network Coffee House and pastor of Urban Mercy—two partner faith communities that share a building near downtown Denver. Both are made up of seekers looking for an embodied, authentic, and more contemplative way of following the path of Jesus. Some of us are agnostic at best, some struggle with addiction more than others, some of us are unhoused, yet all of us are looking for a sense of sacred companionship to navigate the terrain of loneliness.

In these pages, you'll notice a spectrum of influences that range from Kendrick Lamar to Kickback. My wife, Angela, and I moved to Colorado from Indiana in pursuit of a seminary degree. Somehow, I managed to attain that while discovering so much more outside the classroom than I'd ever imagined. I'm also a recent sendee of the Living School for Action and Contemplation, which further shaped my love for the mystics and the practice of contemplative prayer.

But more than anything else, I think you'll notice that the most powerful influences on my life have occurred outside the camp of any formal institution and beyond any semblance of status quo comfort.

I've taken up the invitation an ancient author of a book in the Bible called Hebrews offered. That author put it like this: ". . . Jesus suffered outside the city gate to make the people holy through his own blood. Let us, then, go to him outside the camp, bearing the disgrace he bore."

Outside the camp can be a disorienting wonderland that other authors in the Bible refer to as the wilderness. **A humiliating place.** A place of profound self-discovery. A place where my old maps, resources, and assumptions just don't cut it.

It's a place where I can't seem to fix anything. It's a place of the heart—**a place where God speaks.**

My goal in the following pages is to describe what it looks like to recognize, follow, and be shaped by the sound of the holy that resounds in the wilderness.

It's going to be awkward, so let's be aware of our preoccupation to run off and fix it. May we set our assumptions aside and sink down into an open-hearted walk outside the camp into the holy.

I am deeply convinced that the Christian leader of the future is called to be completely irrelevant and to stand in this world with nothing to offer but his or her own vulnerable self.

—Henri Nouwen

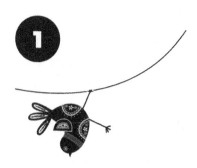

JENGA STEVE
AN UNEXPECTED OPENING

In the beginning was the sound. I can't say I really cared for it at first, but it changed me. That awkward and unexpected sound came with an invitation, an alluring offer to step down from the heights of myself and into the humiliating places of the irrelevant.

Can you hear it too?

How do I describe something that can't be explained with logic? When words fail, we have to get creative, so let's use these wild imaginations of ours. Let's enter into the sound as if it were a dream. This dream starts on Christmas day. You unwrap a small yet wildly delightful gift—a ticket to see your favorite band at the world-famous Red Rocks Amphitheater.

Even though the concert isn't for a few months, goose bumps cover your arms as you anticipate being in that moment. In the coming weeks, you catch yourself preoccupied—drifting in and out of fantasies throughout the work day as you build expectations around what the band will look like in person and how their latest album will stir your soul.

You're well into midlife, but in this whole scenario you don't feel a day over sixteen. Now let's fast forward to the day of the concert. You've been so patient and for the most part composed, but you can no longer hold back your childlike giddiness.

You follow the waving hand of the parking attendant as you pull into Red Rocks Park. The glow of dusk light on the rock formations sweeps you into that other place—a transcendent space. The sound of the band's past albums stream through your car speakers. The whole experience is pure magic.

You start climbing a million steps to get to your seat, the impact of the altitude competing with a hit of adrenaline. As the concert crowd swells, lyrics of past albums fill the atmosphere along with all the familiar scents of beer and puffs of organic clouds. The energy is electric—it's just how you imagined it.

You find your seat, say hello to your neighbors, and settle in as the opening act emerges to kick off their set. You're exactly where you're supposed to be.

Daylight has now faded unveiling a canopy of stars, and the glow of downtown Denver has created the best backdrop anyone could imagine.

The frenzied crowd is on their feet shouting; you're all one collective being. As you anticipate that first chord or vocal, you realize that all the constricting details and stresses of life are nowhere to be found; boy does it feel liberating. Here we go!

Out of the darkness steps a small humble-looking figure carrying a tiny flute. You squint to get a better look. What the...? Whatever this is, it's a complete departure from all those daydreams at work. The ten thousand shouting voices abruptly dial down to a stunned silence.

Birthed out of the quiet grows the haunting sound of that flute as it bounces off the canyon walls—a bizarre melody entirely different from what everyone had imagined.

Soon, the dissonance between reality and expectations gives way to restlessness, and some fans start letting out distasteful boos and creative expletives. Some people are even standing up in disappointment and begin shuffling their way out of the park.

Curious and determined, you stick with it, hanging on that sound, bending your ear in anticipation of what will evolve. The more you allow it to wash over your senses, the more your patience pays off. The subtle and delicate sound gradually wraps itself around something deep within you making its home in your heart. As the surprising intro reaches its close, the rest of the band crescendos into a brand-new version of the music you didn't even know you wanted to hear.

That's how this story begins—with a sound, a mysterious expectation-shattering sound. Sound is about resonance and resonance is how we describe connecting at the soul level. Like a subtle flute echoing throughout a canyon, seldom, if ever, does that sound land on the ear of our soul the way we thought it would.

In the beginning of this journey that unexpected sound came to me through the laughter of Steve Myer. But before I get to Steve, I need to invite you into one more imaginative place. This time let's take a nostalgic visit to the magical land of the mid-1990s.

When I, a long and lanky baby-faced kid stepped foot on the campus of Huntington College in the fall of 1996, I had very little imagination for the soundtrack that accompanies my life today. That naïve eighteen-year-old college freshman had two basic priorities: capture the attention of cute girls and create a name for himself on the hardwood—in a state where basketball players are perceived as gods.

Like many Hoosier teenagers, I'd developed lofty hoop dreams and with a six-foot, six-inch frame, a bulky portion of my self-worth was tightly wound around my ability to shoot a leather ball into an iron cylinder. I was one of those Indiana kids who instead of snuggling a soft teddy bear, clutched my precious basketball when my mom tucked me into bed at night.

An anonymous Sufi mystic once wrote, "For thirty years I sought God. But when I looked carefully, I saw that in reality God was the Seeker and I was the sought."[1]

To put that in terms of my roundball pursuits, early on in the basketball season of my junior year, the Seeker made like Shaquille O'Neal and denied my dreams at the rim. Rejected.

Looking at the intense pressure I inflicted on myself, my failing grades, the fundamentalist religion I'd swallowed whole, and my demeaning old-school coach, I could feel a reluctant yet necessary shift slowly developing inside me.

One day, on an unusually warm November morning, that shift snapped into place. I sauntered into Coach Platte's office and stated my intentions to walk away from the game I loved.

In my young world, leaving basketball was the sound of shattering—a colossal disruption in the trajectory of my life.

How was I, a twenty-one-year-old, supposed to grasp this strange new reality . . . that I was being sought out for a life diametrically opposed to the one that had been unconsciously cultivated in me up to that point?

In the beginning was the sound, and I didn't like it but it changed me. Following that sound drew me away from the realm of perceived credibility and relevance and into the humiliating shadows of the forgotten and irrelevant.

In the following despair-soaked days, I'd take long drives throughout the colorless northern Indiana countryside. It mirrored the gray ambiguity of my interior world and the desperate prayers of my dissolved dreams. I carried only the essentials in the sanctuary of my '86 Honda Accord: CDs by Pearl Jam, Blackstreet, and Jars of Clay scattered across the floorboards, an ever-present plaid Abercrombie & Fitch flannel shirt draped over the passenger seat, and a Bible with a soft pack of Camel Lights perched on top. At age twenty-one, I was a caricature of a '90s alt-rock music video as I sucked down cigarettes and cheap gas station coffee to fuel my angsty prayers and melancholy laments.

Expectations are meant to be disrupted.

My roommate, Eric, had this funny habit. He'd finish reading a book and then emphatically fling it across the room of our apartment with no particular target in mind. "You should read that one, Ryan."

I was perfectly content that night playing Madden NFL '98 when Eric's book took flight and hit me square in the chest. I had never heard of the author, a catholic priest named Henri Nouwen. But upon Eric's insistence, I opened up to the possibility of an entirely new sound.

When I reflect back on my life's journey, I can't help but trace my footsteps back to those awkward days at Huntington when Father Henri's words created an unexpected opening. Quitting the basketball team had severely undercut my self-image, and in the middle of attempting how I might redefine myself, I read the following words.

"I am deeply convinced that the Christian leader of the future is called to be completely irrelevant and to stand in this world with nothing to offer but his or her own vulnerable self."[2]

A new and unexpected sound. Like a door slowly creaking open, Father Henri's words created a deep curiosity within me, and I couldn't help but hear them as a personal invitation.

There was something about Nouwen's life story that enraptured me, that echoed off the canyons of my soul. He traveled a distinct path, descending from the relevance of a sought-after priest and a renown Ivy League professor, to the utterly invisible role as chaplain for a community of disabled adults.

Father Henri sunk further into intimacy with Christ as his relational roots deepened and spread out among culturally irrelevant friends who couldn't care less about his esteemed reputation, successful academic résumé, or the numerous books he'd authored. I resonated so deeply with Father Henri's life and teaching in that unique season of my life that it began etching a tattoo on my heart—one that only seems to become more vivid in sharpness and color as time goes on.

Upon college graduation and newly married, it was time to find that first real adult job. It was Father Henri's influence that led me to accept a position as a case manager for mentally and physically challenged adults. My caseload was made up of a litany of socially disadvantaged individuals who lived with traumatic brain injuries, along with developmental disabilities.

In the two years I occupied that post, just imagine one continual blooper reel of awkward moments. I was Barney Fife[3] patrolling Mayberry with an outdated and defunct pistol at my side.

Please excuse the gun analogy, but the one bullet in that pistol was my willingness to love all types of people. And far too often, that one bullet would get stuck in the chamber or lazily trickle out of the barrel like a tiny ball of Play-Doh.

As I'd meet with my clients to discuss their quality of life, we'd usually break the ice by playing a board game of their choosing. A young college grad ready to conquer the world—one game of Uno and one adult diaper change at a time.

Now back to the sound of Steve Myer's laugh.

Without fail, every meeting with Mr. Myer kicked off with a few beautifully ridiculous games of Jenga. Steve's body wasn't exactly built for a game that requires a steady hand, but there was no convincing him to choose anything else. From birth, Steve's extremities were gnarled and twisted so that his working hand was permanently stuck in a J shape. Four of his fingers crooked backward toward his wrist and a hitchhiker's thumb pointed in the opposite direction. That thumb turned out to be his most effective Jenga finger.

In addition to the tornado shape of his body, Steve also suffered from violent and unpredictable tremors, which without warning, would cause his whole body to drastically jerk. Now, can you take all that and imagine it in the context of a carefully planned and executed Jenga move?

Steve's passionate love for playing the game of Jenga was only outdone by his love of laughter. It didn't take much to tickle his funny bone, and when he laughed it was an unadulterated, full-bodied, earthshaking event. Looking back on this relationship, I have no doubt that Steve was in on the joke—some divine cosmic conspiracy designed to teach me that the divine sound is often hidden within the most awkward and irrelevant of people and places you could imagine.

Steve and I were oblivious to the fact that he was serving as my spiritual director during this vulnerable season of my life. This simple, uneducated man with such limited capacity to control his own body was mystically caught up in God's agenda for my developing sense of intimacy, connection, and awareness.

In the ongoing work of my personal image-maintenance projects, it's been hilarious and humiliating moments with precious image-bearers like Steve that allow me to keep placing my feet back on holy ground.

It's stunning, really. I've been a Christian from the cradle. With an expensive seminary degree and ten thousand hours logged of sermons and Bible studies, I can tell you stories about burning bushes and talking donkeys, yet it's still so hard to stay awake to the sounds of Jenga Steve's laugh in the world—to the **mysticism within ordinary experience.**

The Living Presence of Christ is often so plain, so simple and poor, so seemingly irrelevant, that neither progressive nor conservative minds can manage to recognize the transcendent sound. So many of us see the blocks of Jenga as a game to be won rather than a means for intimate connection.

On the conservative end are those who painstakingly stack their doctrinal, moral, and biblical blocks with a suffocating intensity to ensure the tower doesn't topple on their watch. They peer critically over the rim of their dogmatic glasses at any who approach "the idea of God" differently than they do.

On the progressive side of the table are the sarcastic smarty-pants—those socially woke warriors who arrogantly scoff at their puckered up, piety-obsessed rivals. They can't believe they're stooping this low to play such a childish game against such inferior intelligence.

Let's be honest, who hasn't occupied a seat on one or both sides of those binary approaches? As our ego so desperately seeks to attach itself to a winner, we lose sight of the transformative relationships that are the very presence of Christ in our lives.

Pause and listen.

The music of the irrelevant Christ is resounding even now through unlikely prophets who come to us in the form of friends like Steve Myer.

It's too obvious; Steve wasn't cut out to compete at a game like Jenga. Guess what else is obvious? Many of the folks who skirt the margins of society aren't cut out to navigate the theological or political sparring that take place within our religious and civic institutions.

"The poor are our teachers. We are their students."4 This precept has become more and more true to me over the years. **It's when we lead from our privilege, righteousness or head knowledge that we tend to get it all wrong.**

In the process of playing this ridiculous game day after day with someone so "unqualified," I gradually began to respect who Steve really was, who I really am, and the mysterious disguised forms Christ seems to enjoy taking on in our ordinary day-to-day life. Through saints like Steve, Christ breaks down the soil of my soul to prepare it for the seeds of transformation.

In the beginning was the sound and the sound is meant to echo throughout the canyons of our life, inviting us all into the divine realm of relationship.

Relationships, particularly those among and with the poor, are the mirrors that allow us to see ourselves as we truly are. Relationships humiliate, educate, create, and re-create us.

I'm slowly recognizing that it's the energy of relationship that pulls me through the evolutionary process of becoming my true self. Traditionally, western Christians call this process sanctification.

The Jenga block tower I strive to keep standing at all costs is the very tower of my addiction to certainty, power, and control. Expectations, as I've learned from the mystics, are meant to topple like those wooden blocks.

How would I have known that walking away from my basketball dream at twenty-one years of age was just what this Hoosier boy needed to wake up to the beauty hidden within irrelevance?

These days I'm an evangelist for "wasting" time among the irrelevant ones. As I've encountered the exterior and interior poverties of my life, the towers of my ego continue to fall as Christ offers the terribly liberating truth that I am not Lord of the Universe. In fact, I'm just as preciously irrelevant as Steve.

The Seeker took my busted dreams and re-shaped them into the funky work I do now as a pastor among the street community of downtown Denver. As I allow myself to be in relationship with the marginalized and overlooked, I continue to wrestle with the terrible reality of my powerlessness. Perhaps I'll never readily or fully accept it. But in the wrestling, I keep hearing a distant laughter.

Maybe it's the laugh of God, or maybe it's Steve Myer's still ringing in my ears. Can I accept the reality that Steve's laugh and God's are one and the same? The laughter reminds me that in Christ, all of life is the music of mercy drawing us toward relationship.

I will be waiting here...
For your silence to break,
For your soul to shake,
For your love to wake!
—Rumi

LONGING & LIBERATION
GREEN BANANAS

Looking back on my twenty-three-year-old self is a little like staring at a green banana. It'll ripen eventually.

These twenty-some-odd years later, I suppose I'm more yellow. And honestly, a few humbling dark spots are beginning to show. All I can do is laugh at where I've ended up.

If I could go back and tell that young man just how much those ordinary games of Jenga would become a metaphor for my life's work, I'm sure I'd have jumped up and ran screaming for the door. There's a good reason we start out green, develop slowly, and can't often see beyond the end of our nose along the way.

As I reflect back upon those days with Jenga Steve, I can't help but pour out a tall glass of humility and drink deeply. My body language was all fingers tapping impatiently on the table while the other hand propped up my sleepy head. "What a colossal waste of time," I remember thinking as I sat there anticipating the next tumbling of blocks and Steve's ensuing fit of laughter. "Surely, I'm destined for something more impressive than this!" Steve wasn't even capable of tagging me on social media back then to let the world know how wonderful a friend I was.

Now, in these more yellowed years, the game of Jenga has morphed into chess, and time spent with Steve has been replaced by friends like Rob Dogg and Reggie. But thankfully, the humble wisdom that flows my way through these friends remains just as powerful.

I wouldn't change it for the world.

In our eclectic little downtown coffeehouse we practice the same remedial work of simple presence. As we hang around, our relationships deepen through the mysterious daily rhythm of showing up and waiting with each other and God.

"Only in returning to me and waiting for me will you be saved; in quietness and confidence is your strength . . ."[5]

I'm slowly learning that in all the re-turning and seemingly pointless waiting there's more than just coffee brewing here. What's really percolating are the sacred yet ordinary relationships that draw forth a spiritual re-birth. Our sense of awareness and appreciation for overlooked beauty gradually awaken here.

What exactly are we waiting for? The responses to that question are as varied as the backgrounds, ethnicities, and personalities who dwell inside of the three-story Victorian house on the corner of 14th and Pearl streets in Denver. It's been home to the Network Coffee House for over three decades.[6]

Let's step inside and I'll show you around what we call the Living Room of Christ. First, we'll part the perpetual curtain of cigarette fog as we walk up the front steps to the porch and pull open a heavy wooden door with a stained-glass window.

Immediately, a distinct scent hits your senses and you see my face light up as I bark out, "Yo! What's happenin' today, Reggie?"

"I'm just waiting for that breakthrough, man," he says with a grin on his face and a twinkle in his eyes. That's our resident sensei, Reggie, a native of Denver in his mid-fifties who so consistently offers a calm smile and a peaceful presence that it tends to dissolve all our fears.

Waiting for that breakthrough. . . . And who among this ragamuffin congregation isn't waiting for some form of breakthrough?

Now stroll up to the bar with me—it looks like it's made of an old bowling alley lane—and help yourself to a cup of coffee in one of our fine china cups. If they seem more like a mismatched collection of donated ceramic mugs, you wouldn't be wrong. Don't forget a healthy dose of sugar and powdered creamer so you get the full experience.

Here at Network we sip on subpar, yet sacramental coffee, we take our chess matches just a bit too seriously, and we stumble through earnest childlike prayers as we collectively wait for that elusive breakthrough.

From across the room a voice is lobbed in my direction, "Pastor Ryan, you got time for a haircut today?"

Greg, a freckle-faced twenty-six-year-old with a disheveled mop atop his head, spends most days strolling up and down a five-block stretch of East Colfax Avenue panhandling for just enough money to score some weed and a couple of 18 oz. cans of malt liquor for himself and his five-man crew, whom we affectionately call "the posse." On this day I oblige, so Greg carries a chair out to the parking lot behind our building and plops himself down like a sack of potatoes. I unwind an extension cord, plug in the clippers, and turn them on. Like a bell to one of Pavlov's dogs, the click and hum of the electric trimmers is this lonely introvert's cue to start talking.

"I need to get inside this winter, Ryan, no joke. And I need to find a job. Could you toss up a prayer for all that?"

Since the last haircut, Greg's been saving up a handful of vulnerable confessions for me because you just can't speak this openly around your crew on the street.

"Have you spoke to your parents lately?" I ask.

"Actually, I'm saving my money for a Greyhound to go visit 'em."

In a previous parking lot barber session Greg mentioned the decade-old rift between him and his parents and how any reconciliation hinges on their long-awaited contrition. "I've waited ten damn years on a simple apology, man."

Ten damn years. Waiting for a breakthrough.

I shake the remaining hair off my shirt and step back into the coffeehouse as my eyes pan across the crowded room of familiar faces. I easily identify one personal story after another of waiting.

Have a seat. Let me point out a few of the folks and their stories.

The black bald baritone over there is Red. He's growing predictably grumpy as he waits on that first-of-the-month government check. "At this point it's just a waiting game, Ryan." That's Lisa's line as she miserably endures her final days amidst the advanced stages of AIDS.

Darrel makes it inappropriately clear to our female volunteers that he's just waiting to get laid again, while Ricochet slyly schemes for his next drink as his buzz wears off.

As they wait, most within our community simply can't afford the veneer of middle-class politeness. The aroma of coffee and musty bodies fills up this sanctuary every day with a wildly authentic, sometimes bitter, yet always grounding cup of real life.

It's the cup Jesus drank from.

Thomas Merton said, "My life is measured by my love for God, and that, in turn, is measured by my love for the least of His children. And that love is not abstract benevolence: it must mean sharing their tribulation."[7]

How do we share in the tribulation of the so-called least? Those of us sporting our middle-class blinders who reside within insulated silos of privilege may not have the faintest idea how.

If you're reading this from a rural farmhouse in Iowa, let me clarify something. **The invitation is not specifically to seek out a life among the urban poor. The invitation begins right where you are, by becoming present to yourself. Only when we're acutely aware of our own poverty and loneliness (and those most painfully dissatisfying parts of ourselves), will we awaken to the healing presence of Christ. The longing and the liberation—the personal process of waiting—appear distinct from person to person.**

In becoming present to yourself, imagine clothing yourself in a grace-infused self-awareness that can withhold criticism and judgment long enough to observe how we react to our own experiences of waiting, suffering, or grief. Let curiosity replace fear or pain. That non-judgmental inner observer is the very Spirit of Christ actively and lovingly drawing you into your most transformed, ripe, and true self.

With that in mind, I invite you to pause and seriously consider this question: What is your *heart* waiting for? I'm not talking about the next iPhone or the illusion of the next elected politician who'll finally set our minds at ease. Just like Jesus implored the fishermen,[8] I urge you to go further out and deeper down.

Peer below the waterline of your life and ask, **"What is it that I'm really waiting for deep down in the overlooked corners of my heart?" If we can let this question access our heart, it opens a sacred window that allows the light of our deepest yearnings to shine in.**

For me? I've been waiting nearly a decade to complete this damn book and see it published! I have great friends, who I visit regularly, who are waiting to die and other friends sitting in a prison cell waiting to be released. And then there are those people in my life who have been relationally hurt, and together we're wading through the process of reconciliation. Waiting stinks; but seen through the eyes of our heart, something deep within tells us that it's not pointless.

One of my spiritual teachers, Cynthia Bourgeault, remarks, "As we enter the path of transformation the most valuable thing we have working in our favor is our yearning."[9]

Waiting taps into our holy desires—our deepest yearnings.

Vinny is a deeply thoughtful Lakota friend who you'll hear more about later. Currently, he's serving a twenty-five-year sentence in a high security prison a couple of hours south of Denver. In his most recent letter to me he profoundly reiterates Cynthia's words above when he writes, "One thing that waiting does is bring your true desires into focus." Being forced by law into his monastic cell has brought Vinny's yearnings to the surface as he waits.

For most, if not all of us, this hard spiritual work must be forced on us by less-than-pleasant circumstances. Unemployment, addiction, infertility, grief—if we're present to them, the work of waiting leaves no one out.

Those who dwell in the shadows of the culturally relevant wait on public display. These souls have helped me see that all of us live within an unfinished story. They also point me to the theme of waiting threaded throughout all those Bible stories that are caught in the net of my earliest memories.

If you're conscious of the waiting you begin seeing these stories all over the place. Here are just a few.

» There's Joseph and his technicolor dream coat. Amidst the earth-shattering pain of family betrayal, human trafficking, and enslavement, the man waited twenty-four years for his initial dreams (of bundles of grain and heavenly bodies and stars bowing before him) to make any sense.[10]

» Then of course, there's Abraham. The Father of our Faith waited twenty-five years for the birth of his son, Isaac, after hearing God promise that he'd be the patriarch of a family too numerous to count.[11]

» You may also remember that the central story of the entire Hebrew scriptures surrounds a people who wandered and waited forty years for a glimpse of the Promised Land.[12]

» Similarly, Jesus's orientation into a life of ministry began with a period of waiting—a forty-day wilderness boot camp of fasting and shadowboxing with his ego.[13]

Once our attention is brought to it, we begin seeing stories of waiting throughout the biblical narrative and throughout much of our painfully ordinary life circumstances.

I waited patiently for the Lord
He inclined and heard my cry
He brought me up out of the pit
Out of the mire and clay
I will sing, sing a new song[14]

One of my most memorable experiences of "church" occurred on a Denver light-rail after the conclusion of a U2 concert in 2005. It was their Vertigo Tour and Bono and the boys stepped off the stage one-by-one while singing an encore of "40," which is Psalm 40 put to sweet melody.[15]

As they left the stage, the beer-soaked congregation continued singing and singing and singing. I stepped onto a snug and sweaty southbound train while hundreds of us sang that tune at the top of our lungs. I'm smiling from ear to ear recalling being stuck in that transcendent moment.

Speaking of U2's song "40," when it comes to biblical stories of waiting, have you ever noticed how frequently the number forty appears?

Here are a few examples:

» It rained for forty days and forty nights.[16]

» Moses was on Mt. Sinai for forty days and nights.[17]

» The Israelites wandered and waited forty years in the wilderness.[18]

» Jesus waited forty days in the wilderness as he began his ministry.[19]

» There were forty days between the resurrection and the ascension.[20]

After studying the Hebrew scriptures with my friend Alan, who happens to be a Jewish rabbi and one of the most spiritually attuned people I know, I finally asked, "Alan, what's up with the number forty?"

In typical rabbi fashion he responded to my question with a question. "Ryan, how many weeks does it take for a child to fully develop in her mother's womb?"

That would be forty weeks.

Since time is measured in seven-day weeks, the duration of a human pregnancy would have served the Israelites as an easily accessible metaphor for how we transform and deepen our sense of relationship with God as we wait.

As the mother-to-be waits, she is met with the realization that she cannot control the life within her. In many respects it's such a powerless position—a position of faith. And so she dreams. Out of deep love she nurtures the mystery within her. She pays attention and nourishes her body amidst painful stretching, sickness, and often an intense entanglement of feelings—feelings that certainly include disorienting moments of doubt and despair.

This is the reality of waiting.

> » This is freckle-faced Greg as he's panhandling for change.

> » This is Jonah in the belly of the whale as he wrestles with his mission.[21]

> » This is Vince in that prison cell as he does his Lakota bead work.

> » This is my wife, Angela, as she waits for her mother's dementia to take her to her final rest.

> » This is all of us if we nurture the waiting through prayer and stillness.

This is the cosmic pattern for how each of us grows in consciousness and depth.

Each of us exist within the holy mystery of gestation.

Simply by virtue of being born, we receive the universe's invitation to cultivate and prepare a spiritual womb—an interior space of dark stillness. We nurture, nest, and prepare our being in expectant hope that we'll be receptive to the birth of the Christ within—our truest self.

And then, we wait.

The Jesuit priest and paleontologist, Pierre Teilhard de Chardin, offered an appropriate prayer for this mysterious space of gestation: ". . . in all those dark moments, O God, grant that I may understand that it is you who are painfully parting the fibres of my being in order to penetrate to the very marrow of my substance and bear me away within yourself."[22]

Pardon me if I'm over-spiritualizing this. Let me completely disclose the fact that I'm terrible at waiting. Let's not romanticize it. Waiting is about as enjoyable as a rectal exam. But to endure it together with Christ we ask ourselves: **Can we envision all circumstances of waiting as a sacred season of incubation and nurturance of our true self—a self from which a deeper intimacy with Christ and an expanded imagination of the soul can emerge?**

As so many of those biblical stories point out, only within a real encounter with our powerlessness will our false self begin to surrender its grasp on our lives. Waiting acquaints us with our poverty— that fearful child within who is desperately determined to cling to cultural relevance and to maintain control of its own destiny.

Jesus described this sacred process of God's ever-evolving life within us as the paradoxical death of being born again.

In John's gospel, a man named Nicodemus asks Jesus what it takes to see the kingdom of God. Jesus presents this very metaphor of human gestation saying, "no one can see the kingdom of God unless they are born again."[23] Nicodemus, a man of powerful status, simply could not go to those depths. He wanted to know how a person could enter their mother's womb a second time. Jesus had to make it clear that he was speaking of the spiritual birth, which unfolds within us as we learn to humbly rest in the poverty of our waiting.[24]

Christians have long celebrated the bright excitement of spiritual birth while bypassing the dark abyss that allows it. Celebrating Easter with no reference to what happened in the forty days prior is hollow.

When we bypass the invitation to prayerfully wait, we skim over the surface of our own life.

Until I began exploring beyond the evangelical protestant world that raised me, I had no experience or language from the season of Lent. I never considered the symbolism of Holy Saturday, nor the real-life implications. These are the very things that help us understand that doubt and despair are more like necessary traveling companions than enemies as we traverse our intense seasons of waiting.

Sue Monk Kidd knows about waiting. In her excellent book, *When the Heart Waits*, she writes **"Whenever new life grows and emerges, darkness is crucial to the process. Whether it's the caterpillar in the chrysalis, the seed in the ground, the child in the womb, or the True Self in the soul, there's always a time of waiting in the dark."**[25]

As I wait, the varied personalities and circumstances of folks like Reggie, Lisa, and Red mirror hidden aspects of my own personality and prayers. The oft-overlooked individuals within our community of chronically homeless are the words of the Psalms lifted off the pages of a dusty old Bible. So many of these friendships have offered new and deeper insight to my personal experience of waiting.

But lest you think I've gotten better at waiting than the young Ryan (as he waited head-in-hand for Jenga Steve to make his next clumsy move), I assure you that young Ryan is alive and well in the yellower-banana me today. There are plenty of days you'll find me upstairs in my office at Network with my hand propping up my heavy head as I hit the speed bump of my ego wondering, "What's the point?"

I can't change Lisa's diagnosis or prognosis. I can't hasten my dying friend's relief. I can't force Greg to see that apologies usually go both ways, and I can't house him this winter. I can't get Vinny out of jail, nor can I make certain he is never imprisoned again. I couldn't take away my wife's pain as she progressively lost her mother to Alzheimer's over several years.

I am powerless, poor, and thankfully in an evolving, grace-saturated relationship with God and friends of all types. I'm human.

But, intermingled with our waiting are our fixations. We obsess over our phone. We plan our next vacation, pick our nose, and dabble with any other imaginable diversion to squirm away from the invitation to go deeper. We're not elegant waiters.

All waiting is a dark and disorienting womb—a living metaphor for the coming birth of Christ within you.

But as we wait together in our shared glory and poverty, we can trust that there is indeed more to the story. Something redemptive is being divinely woven amidst the painfully awkward, sometimes incomprehensible conversations, seemingly pointless board games, and confounding conflicts. Through it all we can trust that new and deeper relationships are being birthed.

If the beat is time,

flow is what we do with that time,

how we live through it.

The beat is everywhere,

but every life has to find its own flow.

—*Jay Z*

PARTICULARITY & PRESENCE
MOURNING DOVE

It was only mid-April, and so far I had replaced three broken windows at the coffeehouse that year. Two of those were busted by a mentally fragile friend who roamed the streets, and another was broken by a middle-class neighbor who came to complain about our "fuckin' degenerates, bums, and junkies who ruin the neighborhood." At Network it's not uncommon to experience the pressure from both within and without.

It was a rainy Saturday morning, a day after that adrenaline-pumping exchange with the irate neighbor, that I found myself bottled up with suppressed overwhelming discouragement. For the sake of my wife, Angela, and our boys, I decided the best move for me on a morning like this would be to get my ass upright, change clothes, and go for a hard run through the neighborhood. My innards were a twisted ball of frenetic dark yarn, tangled with feelings of rage, and at least a few threads of despair. Those emotions, along with Kendrick Lamar's latest album, had my legs moving and my face furrowed in hopes of sweating the tension out of me.

The last mile of my neighborhood jog typically ends up with a cool-down walk through the tranquil campus of a nearby catholic seminary. Not only is the campus home to one of my favorite stations of the cross, there's also a massive sycamore tree that equally captivates me. I go there to be grounded by those statues and giant roots.

After the type of exertion that makes your brain tingle a little more than it should, I collected my breath by paying both the stations and the sycamore a brief visit. Still feeling impossibly restless though, I exited the seminary grounds and started the four-block walk west toward home.

A couple of blocks away from our house something seized my attention, deftly dissolving Kendrick's rhymes and my hazy fog of despair. It was so delicate yet profound that I removed my ear buds for a closer listen. That something was the gentle cooing of a mourning dove that was regally perched on the electric line directly above me.

A momentary respite from my sour mood, I paused, appreciating her quiet presence and sweet song, then I continued on my way. I don't know how to describe what happened next, but that dove must have been an expert angler. As I attempted to walk on, after about twenty paces, she set her hook in my heart and began reeling me back. It's like she gently but firmly said, "Hold up. Respect me."

Respect.

The Latin origins of the word respect mean "to look again."[26] She made such a remarkable impression on me that a sacred double take was the only appropriate response. Call me crazy, but I'm convinced her tiny elegant-looking face was deliberately fixated on mine.

Doing my best Mary Oliver impression, I let myself sink into the extraordinary mysticism of the moment, that is, until a pick-up truck turned the corner and headed in my direction.

"Be cool, Ryan."

My fragile little ego was afraid of being busted admiring the bird, so I instinctually played it off by bending down and acting like I was tying my shoe. Then I stood up and kept walking.

When the truck moved out of sight, I looked over my left shoulder to re-respect her, and wouldn't you know, the bird turned herself around in order to face me yet again. I was her subject, and this time, I owed her my full, committed attention. I stood there staring upward, attempting to reciprocate that intense gaze. By the time I clearly recognized it as a gaze of divine affection intended particularly for me on that spiritually overcast morning, the whole affair was over.

A common mourning dove—a winged saint with a brain the size of an orange seed—had re-connected me to Divine Presence. She took me by the hand, touched my restlessness and despair, and led my anxious spirit back home.

Upon returning to the house, I plopped down on the floor and started sketching that scene in a notepad. My boys, Josiah and Micah, flanked me on both sides, fascinated by my drawing. Maybe the energy they experienced from me was a bit like what the disciples noticed on Jesus's face when he came down from the Mount of Transfiguration.[27] As I sketched, Josiah looked at Micah and exclaimed, "Dad must have seen God in that bird." He was right, only I'd rephrase it by saying I felt like I was *seen* by God through that bird.

My earlier thoughts regarding the knuckleheads who broke our coffeehouse windows turned softer, empathetic, and even forgiving. My perspective toward my own inner critic turned toward grace as well.

As a fan of Thomas Merton, I couldn't help but wonder if my Saturday morning encounter with the dove was similar to his famous experience on the corner of Fourth and Walnut Streets in downtown Louisville.[28] Or perhaps this is the kind of fire that burned within Teresa of Ávila when she said, "A soul which gives itself to prayer, either much or little, should on no account be kept within narrow bounds."[29]

The mystics, regardless of the era in which they dwell, each embody the desire to see the world through the eyes of divine love.

There are moments when God touches the eyes of our imagination, when anything and everything becomes enchanting. One thing that mystics such as Merton or Teresa of Ávila seem to be saying in unison is that the primary evidence for our Christian faith is that you see Christ everywhere you look. In his book, *The Universal Christ*, Richard Rohr says, "When you look at any other person, a flower, a honeybee, a mountain—anything—you are seeing the incarnation of God's love for you and the universe you call home."[30]

I was graced that morning by an incarnational touch—a healing warmth from some primal cosmic campfire. I felt compelled to direct

that energy toward attentiveness and offer the sacred double take. This re-respect allows seemingly irrelevant objects to transform into extraordinary subjects which captivate, remake, and guide our consciousness back to relationship. I call this metamorphosis from object to subject the work of subjectification.

Perhaps this is the same energy that would overtake the late Mary Oliver when some enchanting scene unfolded, provoking her to flip open her journal and begin composing the poem that became "Such Singing in the Wild Branches."

> First, I stood still
> And thought of nothing.
> Then I began to listen.
> Then I was filled with gladness ---
> and that's when it happened,
> when I seemed to float,
> to be, myself, a wing or a tree –
> and I began to understand what the bird was saying,
> and the sands in the glass stopped...[31]

My Mary Oliver moment came on a drizzly spring morning in which a depressive weight made me feel as if I had no choice but to intensely exert myself while Kendrick's flow helped surface my suppressed inner rage. The howling hurricane of my interior was then absorbed, and at least slightly transfigured, by the presence of an animal about half the height of my size thirteen Nike boats.

If you know Jesus's preferred illustrations for transformation, it shouldn't be any surprise that it's the small and seemingly irrelevant stuff of life that set our feet back on the ground: mustard seeds, a little yeast in the dough, and the presence of children. These easily overlooked gifts call for our respect and invite us to turn down the dial of our frantic mental metronome.

Allowing this encounter to take place were undoubtedly practices like engaging in daily contemplative prayer, exercising regularly, and steeping my spirit in writers like Mary Oliver and Pierre Teilhard de Chardin.

I stand six feet, six inches tall and weigh 230 pounds, but like a small stone shot from a humble sling, the presence of that bird flattened me to the ground that morning. Her presence spoke words my soul was thirsting for like *pause, pay attention, breathe deep,* and even *make room for more joy.* In the midst of our poverty, if we can allow for a still point of attention, sometimes we'll find all the necessary ingredients for seeing ourselves in a unitive relationship with everything.

De Chardin called this reality the divine milieu in his book of the same name. **"However vast the divine milieu may be, it is in reality a centre. It**

therefore has the properties of a centre, and above all the absolute and final power to unite (and consequently to complete) all beings within its breast. In the divine milieu all the elements of the universe touch each other by that which is most inward and ultimate in them."[32]

In Christ we touch upon a universal consciousness. If we believe in resurrection, then we believe there are no limits as to what or who God's saving grace might embody. In the scriptures, the Christ came to Mary disguised as a gardener,[33] the Christ came to two men on the road to Emmaus in the form of an unassuming stranger,[34] shall I go on? There was Balaam's talking donkey,[35] Moses' burning bush[36] . . . so, why not a mourning dove perched on a wire just three blocks from my home?

To repeat de Chardin's last line, ". . . all the elements touch each other by that which is most inward and ultimate in them." Or as the Psalmist says, "Deep calls to deep."[37] And so we slow down and learn to habituate the sacred double take so that even when the alternator goes out during a snow storm, or the mother-in-law criticizes your parenting, you don't become so hooked on your anger and resentment that you're unable to listen attentively to the Living Sound in the form of a dove's gentle song.

It seems the Creator is not much into monologues.

After several years of marriage, I've slowly begun to see that monologues don't tend to lead toward relationship. It seems that an ongoing, deep relationship with the Living Presence comes through an openness to dialogue with all that lives.

When we narrow down any aspect of creation into a consumeristic commodity, we end up giving the cold shoulder to the very Creator who invites us into ongoing dynamic conversation. Creation was never meant to be objectified for our exclusive use. All signs of forward movement in Christ are a movement from objectification to subjectification.

Several years ago, some pastor friends invited me to participate in a three-day workshop intended to help their church develop a vision and strategy for becoming more united with their neighbors. During three full days of lectures and team-building exercises, the facilitators encouraged the clergy and civic leaders to become more creative and to expand our traditional methods of connecting with each other. After a busy day of well-prepared presentations and lots of strategic chitchat, the workshop facilitators invited us to conclude our time around some good wine and unpronounceable hors d'oeuvres.

After about twenty foggy minutes of droning pretense and small talk, the introvert in me started looking for any excuse to shuffle away.

I needed a breather. I excused myself from the hobnobbing and took a moment to stand back and observe the room. That's when I noticed the quiet, pleasant-looking gentleman standing behind the table of wine bottles. As a part of the catering team, his job was to pour out glasses of wine upon our request. His presence was about as subtle and easy to overlook as that of the mourning dove, and just like the dove, something about him drew me in.

He was a middle-aged Latino man earning a living as a caterer in a suburb of Dallas. I didn't know his story, but a strong curiosity compelled me to move in his direction and exchange a hello. I gulped down the remainder of my glass and proceeded to make his acquaintance.

"Thank you for serving us today. How long have you been doing this work?"

The look on his face told me it was highly unusual that anyone from a room like this would break away to interact with him. He responded, *"Lo siento, señor. Yo no hablo inglés."*

I saw this as my opportunity to cash in some of my go-to phrases from high school Spanish class; however, in my attempt to ask the man for his name, I clumsily told him that I loved him. It turns out that the quasi-Shakespearean question, how do I love thee? (*¿Cómo te amo?*) is pretty similar to, what is your name? (*¿Cómo te llamas?*) in

Spanish. Fortunately, he knew what I was trying to ask, and we both enjoyed an awesome cross-cultural chuckle at my expense

From there we both earnestly and awkwardly went back and forth with broken Spanish and English like a couple of toddlers learning to communicate with words and facial expressions. We were at least able to offer our names, some personal background, and a basic blessing.

I was delightfully caught off guard by his name, which happened to be the very ordinary Spanish name Jesús (hay-SOOS).

A while later, I met up with my friends again. As we took a few steps outside of that hotel conference room, the reality of my little exchange with Jesús caught up with me like an unexpected tickle. I laughed out loud. Amidst all the white male homogeneity, and all the energy expended to generate greater unity, there stood Jesús in a quiet corner of the room.

Of course he would be disguised as an immigrant working for a catering company, and of course he'd be unceremoniously refilling our wine glasses! What else should I expect?

The song in the letter to the Philippians said that Christ took on the form of nothing.[38] **The reason we don't typically spot the divinity within our ordinary experiences and relationships**

is because there's nothing extraordinary to see. Seldom do I discover any immediate hit of adrenaline or euphoria within the places and people Christ hides.

Perhaps part of the reason we're so apt to objectify our relationships solely for our personal benefit, is our tendency to envision the world in bland, broad generalities—such as "all Christians are homophobic" or "all squirrels are narcissists."

The moment we lose the one in the faceless many, we lose divinity. The power is in the particularity.

Take clouds for instance.

On a bright, blue-sky day, stretch yourself out on the grass while looking up at the slow-moving puffy clouds. As you lay there looking up at the blue-and-white-splotched canopy, take a few deep breaths. You see various collections of beautifully enchanting clouds. Now, I invite you to shift your perspective and focus on one singular cloud. Pick one out—one singular cloud. Be careful not to hurry through this exercise. If you feel compelled to capture this cloud with your camera, go ahead, because you may want a visual reminder later.

Now, back to the subjectification. Take in the cloud's form and movement. Recognize that God is choosing this to exist. Now there are no longer a mass of clouds, rather there is only *this* cloud. Do you notice the association between particularity and Presence?

With true sight we recognize that the world is comprised entirely of this-ness—this bird, this cloud, this woman, this man, and even the things I love to hate, like this discarded cigarette butt and this dirty dish on the counter.

This is what makes our work at Network, our small living room coffeehouse for the marginalized homeless, so important. Because we are on a small, relationally-focused mission, we engage in the particularity of the person. When we're doing our work well, we notice patterns that trigger anxiety in Zeke, and other movements that make Kickback laugh. We can easily distinguish Crystal's high-pitched trill laugh from Sam's hearty chuckle. We don't even have to be looking at them to know who is who because no two laughs are alike. After a while, there are no longer homeless people there. It's just Mary, Clint, and Rob Dogg. They're like doves, quiet caterers, and clouds inviting our attention to the miracle of their particularity.

The future of relationships on planet earth— not only human relationships, but relationship with every created species—depends on how we cooperate with God in refining our practice of subjectification.

This is what God is up to. The fact that you just took a breath means that right now God is choosing you. Will you let yourself be seen?

*I am convinced that the universe
is under the control of a loving purpose,
and that in the struggle for righteousness
man has cosmic companionship.*

—Martin Luther King, Jr.

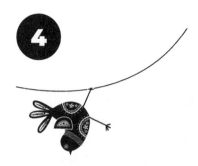

THE DIVINE MORTAR
FRIENDSHIP

"Ryan, how would you summarize your theology?"

Yeesh. If you're gonna open up a Q & A session with a large group of college students, I suppose it should be no surprise that this would be the first question.

"Friendship."

That one-word response spilled out quite naturally.

There was a time, of course, when I would have forced a fancier, religious, or more intellectual response like "incarnation" or "resurrection," but surprisingly, the first word to surface was one that is commonly understood by all people and cultures throughout our planet.

Healthy friendship transcends concepts like religion, ethnicity, and sexuality, and I believe it to be the divine gift at the heart of any family or community who embodies God's infinite love.

"I no longer call you servants . . . instead I have called you friends"[39] Jesus remarked to his disciples—who after three years of relationship had become accustomed to appropriately identifying him as Teacher. According to Jesus, friendship appears to be the omega point[40] (final point of unification) in the evolution of our work and relationships.

It never ceases to surprise me when one of our guests takes a pit stop through Network's living room just to experience the aroma of friendship through the simplicity of a conversation or a quick hug. "I just stopped in to see you, brother!" Wayne said as he locked up his bike. These words warm my soul, but they also confirm the stark difference between outward works of charity and dynamic communities of relationship. **Authentic hope results from the possibility and eventual healing bonds of friendship.**

I'm convinced that at the root of all societal sickness is an epidemic that touches each one of us—loneliness. At this moment, there's a teenager nearby staring longingly at their glowing rectangle waiting for likes on Instagram. Down the street, there's a widow peering out the window of a nursing home whose only child lives three states away. And somewhere in your city is a pastor, with the perfect-looking spouse and three beautiful children, who is secretly gay. Society is soaked with a loneliness that drives the human family toward all varieties of despair and destruction.

This is why communities like Network exist.

Our culture at Network carries the belief that in a society permeated with loneliness, friendship must be the ultimate destination. It's the indicator that detached and damaged people are moving toward healing and healthy attachment. The culture of our community understands friendship like a grand ballroom.[41] If friendship is the ballroom, then service can be considered the hallway. You can't arrive in the ballroom without going down the hallway, but nobody wants to stop short and be stuck in a hallway.

Whether you're on the streets of East Colfax in Denver, a suburban Starbucks, or a quiet rural farming community, it may appear that our primary struggles are against the escalating prevalence of opioids or the evil growing gap between the haves and the have nots.

If we can see below the waterline of these symptoms, we'll discover that their roots lie in the suffering of relational abandonment and loneliness.

Most of our friends around Network enter our community due to a distinct story of painful separation from their family of origin. These beloveds are the separated ones, detached from healthy, meaningful community, and yes, separated from the love of God. The biblical word for this tragic detachment is sin.

When fundamentalists speak of sin, they typically wag their judgmental finger at all those who experience the surface symptoms that offend the fragile sensibilities of the self-righteous. In reality, sin is a collective and fundamental separation—a separation typically traced back to the way the tenderness of a child was somehow disavowed and disparaged.

The Buddhist Master Thích Nhất Hạnh says, **"We are here to awaken from our illusion of separateness."**[42] Waking up to that illusion is no small task within a culture of unhinged capitalism—the kind that sells you the belief "you're simply not enough," that consistently whispers the lie "you're a misfit with a fatal flaw," and that often reminds you "you're not capable of producing the perfection that everyone else can."

Fuck that. It's time to awaken.

The beauty, boundaries, and tenderness of friendship are the antidote for the sickness of separation. I've yet to discover anything that combats the terror of loneliness quite like a collective, cultural pursuit of friendship. These special yet common exchanges, like the above example with Wayne, are a profound reminder that the bricks of any redemptive community are held together by the divine mortar of friendship.

When we reflect upon our best friendships, I believe we'll see them in light of their capacity for compassion. The wise Father Henri reminds us of the same.

> When we honestly ask ourselves which person in our lives means the most to us, we often find that it is those who, instead of giving advice, solutions, or cures, have chosen rather to share our pain and touch our wounds with a warm and tender hand. The friend who can be silent with us in a moment of despair or confusion, who can stay with us in an hour of grief and bereavement, who can tolerate not knowing, not curing, not healing and face with us the reality of our powerlessness, that is a friend who cares.[43]

This is the way of friendship we seek at Network, and I must say that in my experience, dogs are typically far better at this than humans. It's a rare gift to find a soul companion like Father Henri describes, and it should be our life's mission to become this type of friend for others.

The simplicity of sitting with one another in our powerlessness, with no agenda, levels the playing field. It helps us transcend the one-upping games we play as we unconsciously compete for superiority.

I was meeting a friend for coffee in north Denver when a woman overheard our conversation and approached me saying, "I've heard of this coffeehouse ministry you do." I braced for the worst, but I was delighted by what she said next. "That's the place where the lines are blurred between service recipient and service provider."

Booyah! She got it. It's so hard for those unfamiliar with Network not to imagine our work as a traditional soup kitchen for the down and out—one where the dividing line between the haves and the have nots is clearly defined. That's why Network will never really qualify as a service provider. Instead, I hope we'll be known and remembered more like friendship farmers—ordinary people willing to pay careful attention to all four seasons of life, and unafraid to get dirt underneath our fingernails for the sake of redemptive relationship.

Our personal distinctions and diversities are what make friendships colorful and interesting, but it's when we separate one

another as inherently superior or inferior, moral or immoral, that short-circuits the potential for healing union.

Within our community, the sincere hope has always been that we would exist as a safe, down-to-earth hub where our mutuality is clearly seen and celebrated, and we walk away from one another with a deepened sense of solidarity. Over the years, we've begun to see that there is no such thing as Muslim or Christian friendship, gay or straight friendship, white or black friendship, Catholic or Protestant friendship.

Friendship is simply friendship. And there's nothing like friendship to dissolve the dualistic divisions that toxify our diabolically divided world.

In my life it's been my cross-cultural friendships that have served me like a strong cup of dark roast—to awaken my senses and open my eyes to the illusion of superiority and separation.

Vince and Sharon's light-hearted Lakota smiles met me on a hot Wednesday evening in June. They both grew up on Pine Ridge Reservation, about a six-hour drive from the downtown Denver streets where we first met. Vince and Sharon, along with many other Native friends, often testify how life on the streets of Denver has been far kinder to them than life on the "rez."

Shortly after meeting Vince he said, "If we're gonna call you *kola*, I need you to come visit Sharon and I at our home." I soon found out that *kola* is Lakota for friend, and home was under a bridge on the bank of Cherry Creek where they resided with several other urban campers.

On a Saturday morning in September, I awkwardly waddled my way under the bridge with my hands full of breakfast sandwiches and a couple of gallons of coffee. Vince couldn't believe his eyes and his mouth gaped open in shock that I had actually shown up. Sharon's delightful laugh let me know I was in the right place as Vince belted out, "*Hola, Kola!*[44] Welcome to my side of the tracks, homie!"

As folks were shaking off their hangovers, Vince and I passed around cups of piping hot coffee and Burger King egg sandwiches. The vapor of gratitude and grace was as thick as the cigarette smoke as we sat in the divine freedom of being completely ourselves. Underneath that bridge, amidst the potpourri scents of unbathed bodies, alcohol breath, and car exhaust, the *Wakon Tonka* (Lakota, for Big Mystery) taught me a thing or two about friendship with Christ. The author of Hebrews puts it like this: "Let us, then, go to him outside the camp, bearing the disgrace he bore."[45]

Real friendships invite us beyond the boundaries of comfortable decorum and even beyond our traditional ethical norms. As we sat there sipping coffee and watching the puddles splash down from the street above us, I looked up to see a *No Trespassing* sign on the underpass wall. *Violators Will Be Prosecuted.*

Jesus's philosophy of ethics appears to have been directed by his love for his friends, and he was prosecuted for it to the fullest extent. If his friends were hungry, then breaking the Sabbath was permissible. If his friends were caught up in showing their affection for him, then wasting a lucrative bottle of perfume wasn't actually shortsighted. For Jesus, the rule of law was always directed by his relationships and never the other way around.

Our friendships, especially those with the socially powerless and marginalized, will never cease to stretch us out like Jesus's arms on the cross. You'll be caught between two thieves, then invited to sincerely love them both. This is the path of salvation, and Jesus reveals that the cost is no joke. Ask Bonhoeffer.

Abraham knows this cost of friendship as well as anyone in the scriptures. He was considered God's BFF. ". . . Jacob my chosen one, descended from Abraham *my friend* . . ."[46] This friendship with God invited Abraham to leave behind the comforts of his family of origin along with the insurance of their wealth and security. It also required extreme patience as he waited twenty-five years for his promised son. God was patient with him amidst many ups and downs, and Abraham stuck with God. This fascinating union between God and Abraham is expressed again in 2 Chronicles. ". . . And did you not give this land forever to the descendants of *your friend* Abraham?"[47]

The word for friend here is the Hebrew word, *ohabka*, a verb meaning "an active covenantal love."[48] The first time this idea of love is mentioned in the scriptures is in Genesis 22:2— take now your only son whom you love (*ahabta*) and offer him as a burnt offering. *Ahabta*, meaning an active covenantal love, contains the same root word as *ohabka*.

What does this archetypal relationship between God and Abraham unveil for us about friendship? Friendship in this context is a deep covenantal love which gives the term "friend" serious weight. When we think of Abraham giving Isaac back to God,[49] we conclude that "legit" friendship is truly initiated when you give something back. The gift of friendship blooms forth as a sacred reciprocity—an intentional giving back and forth. When I say, "I'm going to empty myself out for your sake," and you reply "Right back atcha, pal. I'm going to empty myself out for you," then we've set the covenantal love of friendship in motion.

There's a sacred trust in the mystical "enoughness" that exists in the space between you and me. There's an abundance

of redemptive energy, and we're able to relax into it without fear of it running out. This is a friendship born of covenantal love.

God revealed this omega point through the process of relationship with Abraham, just as Jesus did through the process of relationship with his disciples.

Of all the gifts we've been granted, I'm convinced that the whole-making energy within friendship is one of God's best ideas. The late Celtic poet and theologian, John O'Donohue, describes this energy so beautifully in his classic book *Anam Cara*.

> In everyone's life there is a great need for an *anam cara*, a soul friend. In this love, you are understood as you are without mask or pretension. The superficial and functional lies and half-truths of social acquaintances fall away, you can be as you really are. Love allows understanding to dawn, and understanding is precious. When you are understood, you are at home. Understanding nourishes belonging. When you really feel understood, you feel free to release yourself into the trust and shelter of the other person's soul. . . . This art of love discloses the special and sacred identity of the other person.[50]

The divine gift of friendship leads us to reconciliation and healing because the emphasis is on mutuality. We're in this together. There are no greedy power plays at work, just a reciprocal outpouring of love and trust.

What does that look like? We find other wonderful examples of this mutuality throughout the scriptures, such as Ruth and Naomi, and David and Jonathan, which offer even richer context for this divine relational gift. They're inspiring and they truly embody O'Donohue's description of soul friend.

My friendship with Vince and Sharon compelled me to understand their history, so I decided to visit the South Dakota reservation where they grew up. A friendship forged on the streets of Denver led to a soul-awakening adventure on the Pine Ridge Reservation, which profoundly shaped my perception of US history. Over the course of that weekend on Pine Ridge, I found myself caught up in a powerful sweat lodge ceremony and later using sage and anointing oil to pray for a family's healing.

Are you seeing a recurring theme here? All these uniquely awkward and vulnerable relationships have led me further into the heart of God, which not coincidentally, is the very heart of relationship.

Steve Myer, all those guys in Denver who have taken the risk to sit in my barber chair, Jesús in Dallas, Vince and Sharon—these special relationships have been my ongoing teachers in the seminary of life as I pursue a paperless PhD in the gift of sacred friendship.

As I reflect back, I'm in awe at how one friendship has often led to another. Because of my friendship with Christ, which was encouraged by loving parents, I eventually pursued friendships with Denver's marginalized homeless. And through those friendships, I connected with Vince and Sharon. And that friendship, forged under bridges and in the confines of our little downtown coffeehouse, led me to Pine Ridge where I met Bernard, Cody, and others. And each of these friendships is like a circle dance[51] pointing me back to an even fuller and more expansive friendship with Christ.

The perpetual flow of the circle dance is modeled through God's Trinitarian shape and creates an energy of childlike curiosity. In that state, you see the potential for making new friends everywhere you go. What a beautiful way to combat loneliness.

Naturally, there are varied dimensions to our friendships. I know the depths of some friend's lives more than others, and I have more than a few friends that I'd be hesitant to share my home with. Nonetheless, all friendship is pure gift and opens my consciousness to see the diversity of God.

In a sense, all friendship is friendship with God. Pause your reading for a moment to consider this question: What difference would it make in your day-to-day interactions if you were able to perceive all relational energy as energy returned to the Source from which it came?

As is mentioned at the beginning of the chapter, by the end of Jesus's earthly relationship with his disciples, he proclaims that the relationship had evolved from rabbi to friend. That relationship, like any relationship, had to slowly turn—as on a holy rotisserie—in order to arrive on the sacred plate of friendship.

According to Pierre Teilhard de Chardin this is the natural trajectory of divine relationship: **"God does not offer Himself to our finite beings as a thing all complete and ready to be embraced. For us, He is eternal discovery and growth. The more we think we understand Him, the more He reveals himself as otherwise. The more we think we hold Him, the further He withdraws, drawing us into the depths of himself."[52]**

At the coffeehouse, our metrics of success have to be measured a little differently. The majority of our community carry more trauma, addiction, and crossed-up chemicals in the brain than one could possibly imagine. The success metrics among severely detached people is defined within the work of friendship. As Christians, rather than getting folks to follow a dogmatic step-by-step process toward some idealized salvific moment by praying a magical formulaic prayer, instead we prayerfully reflect on the trajectory of our relationships.

» Is he coming back to see me after a conflict?

» Is she showing signs of trusting my voice?

» Is there evidence for a developing mutuality?

When precious characteristics like these begin to consistently show up in relationship, we know it's cause for celebration. When hints of friendship emerge, we join in the Trinity's joy-filled dance knowing we're moving in the direction of the omega point.

God comes to us disguised as our life.

—Paula D'Arcy

A CREATIVE UNFOLDING
WATERLINES

On an overcast January morning Miss Oneta greeted us with tears trickling down her petite face as she stood on the porch of her empty beige house in the Ninth Ward. I can still see the distinct waterline running across the wooden siding like a recent war wound. About five feet above the foundation of the porch, the waterline remained, an enduring vestige of Hurricane Katrina's devastating visit to the city of New Orleans.

About a year after the hurricane, I had the opportunity to take several trips to the Big Easy. There, I participated in relief work and got to know the heart of that place through folks like Miss Oneta. Those trips to New Orleans quickly taught me how important it is to keep my eyes open so I can see below the waterline of society and myself.

In August of 2005, mother nature wrote one of her harshest exposés. She revealed what was beneath the waterline of that city; the poorest neighborhoods seemed to be strangely, if not strategically, nestled up against the weakest of levees. She also exposed what was beneath the waterline of our federal government, as head-scratching delays prevented emergency relief work and left the many people who lived below the poverty line to fend for themselves.

The severity of poverty in that place left my head spinning, but it was the poverty, along with the depth and beauty of the culture and its people, that captured my heart.

As I hadn't yet settled into the Network community in Denver, Angela and I seriously considered relocating to New Orleans during this period in 2006. After much back-and-forth we decided to remain in the Mile High City, but I couldn't move on from the distinct image of that waterline.

The waterline is a profound symbol within human consciousness. It tells us there's always more to the story of both society and self— more than what we see on the surface.

There's all that we recognize, our conscious awareness, and then there's the entire wonderland beneath that we either cannot or instinctively choose not to see. The waterline points to a timeless truth that is simple enough to be profound: **We simply cannot see what we're not looking for.**

On the morning of January 28, 1986, my mom picked me up from school for a doctor's appointment. As I sat in the waiting room, I couldn't tear my eyes away from the corner television set showing the launch of a space shuttle named *Challenger*. If you were alive at that time then you remember the moment you witnessed that spectacular tragedy. Seventy-three seconds into flight, that extraordinary rocket burst into flames just off the Atlantic coast of Cape Canaveral, killing all seven crew members. One, Christa McAuliffe at age thirty-seven, would have been the first civilian (and school teacher) to ever go to space.[53]

Many confused and bereft school children watched the nationally televised broadcast that morning as the reality of the explosion dried like wet cement in their minds. After years of investigation, it was eventually determined that the shuttle's fate came down to a faulty rubber spacer called an O-ring, which had never been tested in freezing temperatures. Somehow all the experts overlooked this small, seemingly irrelevant-looking part, which annihilated such a powerful symbol of American progress and patriotism. One chilly morning and one design flaw were all it took to reveal the one thing all those brilliant minds hadn't been looking for.

O-rings matter.

And so does the manner in which we translate the ancient sacred text we call the Bible. Regardless of how familiar you are with the Christian scriptures, you've likely heard of what has become known as the greatest commandment. It emerges when an expert in the Jewish law asks Jesus a pointed question: "Teacher, which is the greatest commandment in the Law?"

Jesus replied: "Love the Lord your God with all your heart and with all your soul and with all your mind. This is the first and greatest commandment. And the second is like it: Love your neighbor as yourself."[54]

Consider Jesus's response to the question of what must persist above the waterline—to love God with your whole self and to love your neighbor as yourself.

As a good American evangelical, I had always assumed that we could efficiently and effectively summarize Jesus's response by placing three subjects in sequential order of priority.

(1) God

(2) Neighbor

(3) Self

First off, God. Any good Sunday school student knows the supreme importance of putting God first in our life. So the noble thing to do, or at least to claim to do, is to put others (our Neighbor) before ourselves. And last, with a purposeful emphasis on last, is the Self. We fear that our ego will sabotage everything, rendering us a selfish, disordered embarrassment—also known as "a bad Christian." It all makes perfect sense within our western dualistic paradigm. We crave the convenient sequence that fits in a tiny booklet so that we can pass it along to our non-religious friends. The only problem is that Jesus, a Middle Easterner, didn't see through our western lenses of sequence and order.

When it comes to the standard translation of this passage in Matthew there's like, a problem, ya know? More specifically, there's a problem with the word "like," as in "the second is like it."

Within this powerful and popular text, the word, "like" appears to be . . . wait for it . . . irrelevant. In the original Greek text, the word "like" is a translation of the Greek word *omoia*.

Omoia is an O-ring.

The Greek word *omoia* in the passage of scripture appears to be nothing more than a rubber spacer—an insignificant part with no bearing on the translation of a beloved piece of Christian scripture.

When I hear the preposition "like," I think of similes—an apple is like a banana because they're both in the fruit family. The problem lies in the often tricky process of taking Jesus's native tongue, Aramaic, translating that into ancient Greek, and then translating the ancient Greek into modern English. At this point, we are a couple of thousand years and three languages removed, so we need to do some research on *omoia*.

The word *omoia* in the context of this verse means "resembling the same force"—as in the second commandment resembles the same force as the first, "love your neighbor as yourself."[55]

We learned the hard way that a better designed and tested O-ring would have saved a lot of pain and suffering. The same might be said for a better translation and understanding of the ancient Greek word *omoia*. The word "like," especially in our day and age, just doesn't convey the gravity of what Jesus was saying when he responded to the expert in the Jewish law. Like is neither a valley-girl-ism or a mere comparison in this verse.

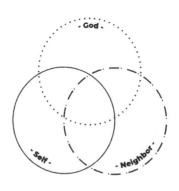

With this new understanding of the translation in mind, the clearly defined sequence of God > Neighbor > Self begins to dissolve. In its place emerges three concentric circles in which our vision of God, Neighbor, and Self equally influence one another within the integrated realities of ordinary everyday life.

Whenever we place a list in a sequential order, a waterline of priority naturally develops. Let's say my wife asks me to go to the grocery store and she hands me a numbered list of items. I have limited time and can only get to the first two items, so the third item in the list falls below the waterline of priority. Think about a pastor, priest, or dedicated volunteer you know. When "life happens" in the God > Neighbor > Self paradigm, self is inevitably deprioritized. I'll spare you the list of ways this goes wrong in ministry and life.

This helps explain the twisted perception of "the self" within much of modern Christian history. We've attempted, albeit with good intentions, to put God first in our life. We've decided the next noble thing to do is spend our energy serving others. But, in the natural process of maintaining our numbered grocery list of religious order, we lost touch with a conscious sense of self-awareness and the transformative power latent within our own story.

When the self becomes a forgotten piece of the equation, it falls below the waterline of our life, and contrary to popular belief, that doesn't result in humility. It actually causes the ego to kick into hyperdrive as it attempts to achieve in order to impress God and neighbor. Why? For the sake of that neglected inner child whose voice became buried far beneath the strata of consciousness. Like the iceberg that took down the unsinkable *Titanic*, we fail to see just how significantly influential the "self below the surface" is. This leaves us lacking and looking, and moreover, it explains why tools like the Enneagram have become wildly popular in recent years.

Christian orthodoxy in general is best understood through the three interconnected circles: Scripture, Tradition, and Experience.

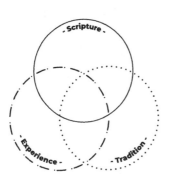

Historically, Protestants have been guided by Luther's agenda of *sola scriptura* and prefer to see through the lenses Scripture > Tradition > Experience, in that order. Most committed Catholics, however, typically prefer the order of Tradition > Scripture

> Experience. While these two different orderings may be perfectly valid, neither give permission to explore our unique psychologies and personalities. Both of these preferences allow the power of personal experience and the awareness of the self to become lost below the surface of what is considered relevant.

Even though we may have been taught how equally interconnected they are, as Christians, we also tend to order the Trinity sequentially: Father > Son > Spirit. The default perception typically seems to place the Spirit last and well below the waterline. Interestingly enough, throughout the scriptures, the Spirit is almost always assigned the feminine gender, and within the historically patriarchal institution of the church, we still haven't recovered from the damaging misconception that the Spirit is intrinscially male.

Sequence and order are vitally important when we're young, but once we emerge into adulthood, we desperately need a non-binary[56] awareness and a non-sequential understanding of reality.

If we're honest, we admit that our craving for order and sequence pervades so many of our efforts at spirituality and life. We try to live as if we're assembling a shelf from Ikea, but no such step-by-step instruction manual exists for daily life.

I believe Paula D'Arcy is right; God truly does come to us disguised as our ordinary life. If you still utter the words "He is Risen" on Easter Sunday, then you must be tuned in to see God in all sorts of disguised forms within everyday life. Mary learned this as she stands outside an empty tomb and fails to recognize Jesus—perhaps because he's wearing a straw hat and holding a garden rake.[57] The two men walking to the town of Emmaus encounter a walking companion[58] who was completely unaware of current events in Jerusalem[59] and he turned out to be the resurrected Christ.

So, when you're behind on your bills and your youngest is screaming about a broccoli situation after your spouse just said something hurtful, it's so easy to overlook the divinity embodied within the encouraging phone call from a friend a mere hour earlier. Invited or not, and whether we're aware or not, Christ is present.

The mysterious energy of resurrection means that there are no limitations to God's presence, and we needn't look further than studying our very own life and its divine moments and trajectories. Your "one wild and precious life,"[60] as Mary Oliver called it, is the deepest and most accessible well we have to draw from in our pursuit of intimate relationship with God.

When we begin to see our life through the non-binary lens of inter-connection, we echo the soul-soothing words of James Finley. **"Although I am not God, I am not other than God. Although I am not others, I am not other than others. Although I am not the earth, I am not other than the earth."**[61]

(You may need to write that quote down like I did and sit with it awhile. The remainder of the chapter will still be here when you're ready.)

Our task then, as we strive to be a people of both prayer and action, is to become attentive students of our environments and the heart of our own experiences—especially those that strike us as awkward, painful, or unfamiliar.

As resurrection people we hold the sense that we participate in the flow of creation within a mysterious, hope-filled, interwoven, and unfinished story. As students of our experiences, we pay attention knowing that it is how we see glimpses of a creative unfolding, even if somewhat veiled.

The mystics have encouraged me to practice being attentive to my own life. The thing about mystics is that as they moved through life, they wrote stuff down. If you fancy yourself a budding mystic (and if you're still reading, then I assume you may) then when you look at your life unfolding, jot it down! I can't recommend it strongly enough. Don't be afraid to document and reflect back upon your experiences like I'm doing in the pages of this book.

I'm convinced that I was prepared for that interior work of reading the mystics and regularly practicing contemplative prayer because I journaled. I can still remember starting to journal one Christmas during college after my grandma handed me a book full of blank pages. It's never too early or too late to start. Like Christ, the blank page meets you wherever you are.

Journaling allows us to see the oft-overlooked patterns and sacred trajectories within our story that we'd otherwise miss. I've been especially thankful that I collected many of my thoughts on paper from three to six in the morning—the hours when we come out of our deepest sleep and into the wild world of our dreams. The Jungian Episcopal priest, John Sanford, calls our dreams God's forgotten language.[62]

In truth, they're the bizarre, sometimes frightening and seemingly irrelevant movie clips in which we are always the featured star. Little vignettes just beneath the waterline of our life can speak such insight and direction into our future if we're willing to pay attention.

Developing our muscles of attention so that we can see and allow ourselves to be moved by our dreams, the simple song of a mourning dove, or the depths of Miss Oneta's tears wouldn't be possible if we didn't feel safe enough to move reflectively through life beyond the pressures of survival mode. Certain pre-existing conditions must be in place to allow for transformation.

In his book, *Essential Teachings on Love*, Richard Rohr breaks it down: "The only people who change, who are transformed, are people who feel safe, who feel their dignity, and who feel loved. When you feel loved, when you feel safe, and when you know your dignity, you just keep growing. That's what we do for one another as loving people—offer safe relationships in which we can change."[63]

The degree of change we are willing to undergo correlates to how deep we are willing to go beneath the waterlines in our life. And our willingness to go there, correlates to the degree we feel surrounded by safe, wise, and loving community.

As I look back at the trajectories of my life, I find that at each vulnerable stage there has been a wise and willing light who has readily affirmed and reassured my steps. Sometimes I've had to seek out these lights after long periods of groping through the dark.

As I was beginning to settle into Network, it was my friend and Network founder, John, who encouraged me to see through the eyes of my heart over infinite veggie pizzas at Angelo's Tavern. Prior to that it was a wildly imaginative minister named Wes, who lovingly pulled my ass, kicking and screaming, through four years of seminary. These days, it's been Penny, Jeff, Scott, Rabbi Alan, and so many other elders who have provided me a scaffolding safe and strong enough to keep growing, changing, and risking the downward descent below the waterline.

Outside of survival mode, when I feel safe and secure in who I am, I can look back with deep gratitude upon the rigid order of my Bible church upbringing that encouraged me to put God first. My initial paradigm of God > Neighbor > Self kept my nose clean and likely saved me from a great deal of hurt during those formative years. Before I could begin to see through the lens of concentric circles, I had to neatly organize my thoughts and ideas into safe boxes. We can only begin to think outside the box if we were graced with a sturdy, well-constructed box to begin with.

So, yes, some things are sequential. Maslow's hierarchy of needs is legit; we can't just miraculously self-actualize or see through the eyes of the mystics unless our basic needs for survival, such as food, shelter, and love, are met.

I'm able to trust my experiences because of a solid education and upbringing in the scriptures along with good training in ecclesiastical tradition. And I'm able to explore below the waterline of status quo society and self because I was gifted a predictably safe childhood home environment. (Thank you, mom and dad!)

That hasn't been the case for a lot of people. My childhood reality is far from the realities of so many of my Network friends who would rather forget what life was like growing up. How can we expect traumatized men and women to experience the reality of God's affection for them and to heal from their real-life nightmares if we don't provide a safe environment, basic needs, and loving kinship?

If God comes to us disguised as our life, then it must be our mission to provide connection and care to society's irrelevant ones who don't feel safe enough to peer below the waterline of their life. With enough safety, prayer, and kindred affection, perhaps they will one day have the courage to see that everything belongs—that even the most terrorizing and shame-filled shit can become the compost necessary for new beauty and possibility.

Waterlines.

We're being invited to take a risk—to go below into that dark abyss of unaddressed grief and unhealed wounds. And we're being invited to risk providing a pathway for others to do the same. Take heart. Christ is there. Love is there. So, down we go!

We're afraid to lose the control we think
we have over the life we think we're living.
—James Finley

6

BLESSED ARE THE AWKWARD
PIMPLES & PARACHUTE PANTS

Anxious? I don't think that adequately describes the feeling I had as I rode the elevator to the top floor of the casino. As the doors were about to part, I still didn't truly grasp what I was doing there.

I suppose I should provide a bit more context.

In early December of 2014 I teamed up with two strangers for what would become a life-altering road trip from Denver, Colorado to Ferguson, Missouri. We were the third trip that year from Denver to Ferguson that modeled ourselves after the Freedom Riders of the 1960s. We set out to connect with both local Ferguson clergy and activists to listen to their stories of struggle and actively join in the protests against generations of police misconduct and systemic racism.

I was so damned uncomfortable with this,
but I knew it was a necessary next step in my
exploration below the waterline of society and self.

The moment I learned that eighteen-year-old
Michael Brown was shot and killed by Officer
Darren Wilson, I found myself immediately
drawn into an awkward, powerless place.
It was the second week in August of 2014. I
looked on as many of my black friends had an
instantaneous visceral reaction that I did not
know how to process. I was sitting in a pew in
Shorter Community African Methodist Episcopal
(AME) Church in northeast Denver the night the
verdict was revealed that the officer would not be
indicted on charges of murder. As the decision
was announced from the pulpit, two young black
mothers sitting directly in front of me began
physically shaking and moaning with wails
saturated in a severely personal pain—a pain I
was embarrassed to be so disassociated from.

That pain disrupted and disturbed me on many
levels. I wanted to understand how they felt.
I had head knowledge of police brutality and
harassment within the black community, but I
had no tangible experience inside myself to reach
back to, no handle for me to grip. My former
sense of solidarity with my black and brown
friends felt suddenly fractured, which created a
troubling restlessness in my soul.

Later that night I left the church and felt compelled to walk downtown near the Denver capitol building. There folks were demonstrating by laying their bodies in the middle of Colfax and Broadway for four minutes, highlighting the four hours Michael Brown's body was left unattended on Canfield Drive in Ferguson.

The scene that night with all its energy had my soul in an inescapable grip. I listened and did my best to take it in, but I knew that just wasn't enough. I needed to involve my body somehow, to pray with my feet, and step into developing my sense of understanding and voice.

These are the circumstances that led to riding that elevator to the top floor of a casino in downtown St. Louis, Missouri. Why the top floor of a downtown casino?

The rapper and entertainer, Nelly, a St. Louis native, was hosting his annual Christmas party in a ballroom overlooking the Mississippi River. The Ferguson collective that I had joined was irately dissatisfied with the wealthy rapper's perceived lack of engagement and commitment to the issues in his native community, and they were about to let him know using bullhorns and direct non-violent confrontation. In that moment my task was to be present to support and participate in their overflowing passion and concern.

Within that cramped elevator of protesters one fellow looked straight at me while asking a friend, "What the hell is *he* doing here?" This was exactly what I had been asking myself as sweat trickled down the spine of my back. And if you don't know me well, then you don't know about my special gift of acquiring a red, splotchy face and neck when my adrenaline and discomfort escalate. Yes, the pale skin with red splotches gave away any hope of hiding my anxiety.

My first priority was to avoid puking on people. That's the level of anxiety I'm talking about.

As we reached our destination, I stepped out of the elevator and into the crowd of about twenty-five Ferguson activists, each dressed in black. The place was mobbed with professional athletes, entertainers, clear skin, tiny party dresses, and sparkly chains.

In a flash, I found myself in the middle of the ballroom lobby among the other activists shouting, *"Black Lives Matter!"* at the top of our lungs. In the middle of the fray stood a six-foot-six-inch Caucasian lightening rod and I suppose it wouldn't have been quite so noticeable if I were dressed in black like the other protesters. But, I still happened to be wearing what I wore to church that morning—tan khakis and a red sweater. I couldn't have been whiter, or redder.

Do you remember Will Ferrell's character as Buddy the Elf?[64] On the top floor of a St. Louis casino ballroom, I completely shattered the awkward-o-meter. And survived.

The morning after Buddy the Elf joined in protesting a St. Louis rapper, my friend Dawn led the Denver crew in a quiet moment of reflection over breakfast. It wasn't until I began to intentionally hear myself express my severe embarrassment, confusion, and discomfort in the sacred company of those friends that the weight of reality truly broke through the confines of my physical body.

Whereas the Ferguson activists felt they had no choice but to be in the trenches to fight for their very survival and the future of their families, I was essentially there to conduct a well-intentioned research project. But because of my exterior pigment, I could have excused myself from their struggle as soon as it became too uncomfortable or inconvenient. The distance between my experience of the moment and theirs was intensely palpable. It all but smacked me in the face.

As we debriefed the events of the prior evening, I pushed my breakfast burrito to the side and allowed myself to melt into a snotty sobbing mess. My generous friends listened as I explained how I had profoundly re-learned that those intense feelings of awkwardness and discomfort were a necessary precursor to any attempt at empathy and solidarity. On my own I could never begin to grasp the ongoing sense of injustice within the black community.

On the journey of solidarity with oppressed people, when privileged folks like me experience awkwardness, it offers a small yet significant window into the ordinary experience of their ongoing suffering. There really is no other way around it. The road toward incarnational presence requires more than just awkward, red-sweater, splotchy-faced moments.

If the process of transformation into the likeness of Christ doesn't provoke a significant degree of interior tension, discomfort, and awkwardness, then I'm afraid I would question the validity of that transformation.

I still struggle to adequately describe how participating in that particular night of civil disobedience in downtown St. Louis changed me, but it did.

For once I wasn't sitting comfortably in the driver's seat. I couldn't pump the brakes and veer left. I couldn't control how people perceived me. James Finley says, "We're afraid to lose the control we think we have over the life we think we're living."[65] That fear and the perception of control are exactly what undercut the white

American church from genuinely loving "the other."

The invitation is to voluntarily give up reaching for any sense of competence and cool knowing that it only gets in the way of consensual vulnerability. Giving up the wheel and shifting over to the passenger seat means that we intentionally remove ourselves from our attachment to personal agency.

Voluntary powerlessness is a necessity for any person of privilege to find their place in the cosmic web of cross-cultural relationships.

The constitution of the alternative universe of Christ, what Jesus typically called the Kingdom of God, is designed to move us beyond personal preference, complacent comforts, and convenience.

If you're like me, having grown up within white middle-class western culture, learning and living this new constitution is like a drawn-out adolescence full of pimples and parachute pants.

Before moving on, I want to clarify two important distinctions within this conversation.

(1) The necessary pursuit of voluntary awkwardness is not an excuse for an adrenaline junkie to go thrill-seeking—hunting down one

humiliating circumstance after another. That's called egoic exhibitionism. It isn't sustainable and it takes you in the complete opposite direction of where I'm pointing. Humility, courage, and discernment will always be the primary ingredients in the pursuit of cross-cultural solidarity.

(2) Do not place yourself in a position in which you feel your safety is severely compromised. It's important not to associate awkwardness with danger, because as an experience of spiritual formation, awkwardness is a place we'll need to return to over and over again.

So, what do I mean by voluntary awkwardness?

Awkwardness is a feeling we all know. You were thirteen years-old once. At the age of twelve I was dealing with a shoe size that matched my age! Adolescence was a time of supercharged development during which the bouncing chemicals and raging hormones knocked us severely off balance. This instability created an in-between or liminal space where our old coping mechanisms and our sense of self-confidence tripped down the rabbit hole into a vulnerable state of disequilibrium.

Thank God we don't stay stuck in teenage adolescence forever. But, when we exit those years, most of us determine never to risk appearing that vulnerable again. Herein lies the problem when it comes to our ongoing spiritual development.

Experiences of disequilibrium create a necessary space within our interior. There, our favorite masks and defense strategies are stripped away so that we stand naked before God—not as who we think we are, but as who we were created to be.

I wouldn't have chosen to participate in that protest if it were on a menu, and I certainly wouldn't have picked out a red sweater if I knew what I was getting myself into. Like Jonah, I had to allow myself to be thrown overboard into the abyss.

We can view this principle of disequilibrium from both a personal and a corporate dimension. It's not hard to see the impact in a peoples' lives (or within any organization or institution) when they've made internal commitments to be guarded or closed off, to play it safe, and to comfortably maintain the status quo. It's hard for me to understand how anyone could be a sincere student or teacher of the Bible and not notice the clear patterns of uncertainty, doubt, and awkwardness throughout the lives of all our flannel board heroes within the sacred text!

If we were to be completely honest about the stories of Abraham, Moses, Mary, or countless others, I think we could create an additional beatitude that says: **Blessed are the awkward for they will find their true self.**

I want to take a brief look at one of the more awkward stories detailed in all four gospels. Entering into this story will work best if you can engage your imagination to see yourself as an actual observer within the story—get in the room with these folks.

The story takes place at the home of Simon the Leper.[66] Jesus was en route to Jerusalem for Passover when he accepted an invitation from Simon for supper. Some accounts mention that Jesus was in the company of friends and disciples. Other accounts make it sound like there were Pharisees and others in the room with whom he wasn't well-acquainted.

At some point during their dinner, a woman with a seedy reputation stood up, began walking toward Jesus, and knelt at his feet to wash them. Much like my casino elevator moment, I imagine someone staring at her while asking a friend, "What the hell is *she* doing here?"

Washing the feet of a guest was customary practice for the host, not a guest. But what this woman did next would have made the most religiously prudent and pious folks squirm completely out of their skin.

First, she started letting her tears fall on Jesus's feet, and then, she scandalously let her hair down and began touching his feet with her hair. This level of intimacy would have certainly transgressed all codes for public displays of affection. As you watch this unfold, look around the room. Picture the expressions on the guests' faces . How does it make you feel? Are you looking for the exit yet? Hang tight; we're not even to the controversial part.

As she tenderly held Jesus's feet, she reached over and grabbed a jar of perfume, poured it out, and began massaging the oil into his feet. The perfume that filled the air with its pungent scent was said to be worth an entire year's salary.

If you grew up in a conservative Christian environment, you know that how *they* spend their money and how *they* handle their sexuality is of chief concern to *us*. This woman's full consciousness was wrapped around her unfettered love for Jesus, which caused her to completely surrender all regard for the other guests' perceptions. Because the others didn't share her sense of utter surrender, she found herself under the heavy weight of self-righteous judgment, and it all made for one supremely awkward scene.

When it comes to understanding her state of consciousness and its effects on others, Howard Thurman provides an excellent explanation.

> **The central element in communion with God is the act of self-surrender. . . . I surrender myself to God without any conditions or reservations. I shall not bargain with God. I shall not make my surrender piecemeal but I shall lay bare the very center of me, that all of my very being shall be charged with the creative energy of God. Little by little, or vast area by vast area, my life must be transmuted in the life of God. As this happens, I come into the meaning of true freedom and the burdens that I seemed unable to bear are floated in the current of the life and love of God. The central element in communion with God is the act of self-surrender.[67]**

When is the last time you've laid bare the very center of yourself so that all of your being is charged with the creative energy of God?

If that question messes with your spirit like it does mine, go ahead and lay down the book to allow the question to fully have its way within you.

That woman in the Gospels, who some believe to be Mary Magdalene, revealed her unashamed affection for Jesus by laying bare the very center of herself. She wasn't carefully gauging the uncomfortable clash between gender, socio-economics, theology, culture, etc. and then calculating her response accordingly. She didn't appear to be concerned with preserving or protecting her reputation or the broader status quo. Paying no mind to the standards of religious or social decorum, her heart was purely surrendered in her love of Jesus.

Wouldn't you love to share that compelling singular focus that she displayed? Me too.

I guess that's what I was doing when I stepped on that elevator. There was an invitation toward self-surrender, that, despite my sweaty back, splotchy face, or choice of sweater, I just couldn't refuse. I was compelled.

What if the experience of awkwardness is a reminder that we're right where we're supposed to be within our growing relationship with Christ? The reality of the Judeo-Christian journey is that we live within an unfinished story. It's unfortunate that we've been coached by culture and religion to interpret "unfinished" as incomplete, inferior, or awkward. It's simply not done unfolding yet.

The beauty of relationships is that they are ever-evolving, and the Spirit of Christ saturates the process. So, slip on that red sweater, lean into the awkward, and lay bare the very center of your being so that you may expand your relational capacity for all people—black, brown, queer, privileged, poor, democrat, republican, documented or undocumented immigrant, and everyone in between.

*All the unhappiness of men
arises from one single fact, that they cannot
sit quietly in their chamber.*
—Blaise Pascal

104

THE DIVINE HEARTBEAT
PRAYER & PUTTY

There's a circular door-knob-sized hole in the wall of my office. Let me share with you how it got there on an otherwise mellow Tuesday morning in the coffeehouse.

I was upstairs attending to emails when suddenly a herd of buffalo came bounding up the steps in a fit of rage. It was my friend Randy. "Where's that tall idiot?" Hmm . . . who in the world could he be looking for?

Randy was experiencing the weight and accusations of the entire universe on his shoulders and he was ready to pulverize anyone willing to challenge him, but in this moment he was specifically hoping to square up with me.

Randy and I have navigated this terrain together before, yet still my gut turned sour with fear.

Randy deals with an explosive bipolar disorder, and in moments like this his reality feels trapped within a bamboo hut in the middle of a Category 5 hurricane. He's starving for someone else's drama to meet his in an epic clash. Cue the outburst.

As he looks at me with murderous visions in his eyes, I know from walking this road before that what he's truly asking for is help getting out of the heat of the moment. He wants a steady presence to firmly, yet calmly invite him into a quiet moment of prayer. Randy is one of those hard-scrabble images of God who has invited me below the waterline of his life. Holding his hand about three feet off the ground, Randy once told me, "Ryan, I haven't been myself since I was this tall. That's when all the neglect, abuse, and rage started."

After an oppressive childhood from hell, Randy spent the next twenty years on the street going in and out of seasons of drug abuse and traumatizing relationships. Through it all he's been one of the most loyal and compassionate members of our community, and he never fails to check in on me, implore me to love my sons, and offer me a solid whoppin' on the chess board. But in tenuous moments like these, I have to invite him to lock in on my eyes as I gently remind him,

"Randy, it's me, your friend."

On this particular day, he just wasn't having it. As he noticed my refusal to join him in the unhinged drama, he stormed out of my office slamming the door backwards, which caused the door knob to lodge into the drywall and form a perfect circular hole. My office wall is now a clichéd paraphrase of Pascal: There is a God-shaped hole in all of us.

In this gig, I've learned that a tub of drywall putty, a four-inch spackling blade, and an ongoing practice of contemplative prayer are all necessary items to keep handy in the ol' toolbox.

The truth is, I experience my own frantic polarities of fight or flight. Although I'm a perpetual beginner at contemplative prayer, practicing it, in combination with effective psych meds, have been my best shot at both mental and physical health.

Fight or flight, or attachment and withdrawal, however you choose to name this instinctive response, should actually be perceived as a gift—a remarkable survival mechanism. It's how our species has made it this far. But in light of complex realities such as climate change and our ongoing struggle with cross-cultural relationships, we're seeing that if we continue to operate in collective survival mode, we're going to be in big trouble. I don't mean to be fearmongering, I just want to see through the lens of reality—and Christians tend to struggle with that.

It's time to transcend the dualities of fight or flight and move toward our deeper longings for connection, depth, and wholeness. I sincerely trust that there's a new consciousness on the horizon and I believe that one of the avenues for growth, healing, and participation is found in an ancient gift called contemplative prayer.

While I don't struggle with severe mental illness, I see such slim distinction between friends like Randy and I when he acts out in a behavioral episode. My fight or flight versions of survival mode are simply more socially acceptable to middle-class sensibilities. It's not as if I don't struggle with compulsive thoughts like incessantly wanting to check sports stats, have a cigarette, or eat my feelings. Are not all of our goofiest behaviors and manic emotional swings a cry for relational connectivity with the Living Presence?

Like Randy, my deepest longing is for a still point of consciousness. I yearn for God to invite me back home so I can I hear the words my heart desires: "Ryan, it's me, your friend." Home is when the tension dissolves and I find myself taking slower and deeper breaths. Home is when I realize I'm completely known and loved in the naked now. Home is rest and union with the Living Presence.

The question is, how? How do we fall into that place of intimate union with God?

When it comes to the traditional idea of prayer, I've prayed so many words over the years— words of blessing, words of thanksgiving, and gobs of desperate petitions. I won't stop any of that, but nowadays my most life-giving practice has been dwelling in the sometimes calming, sometimes terrifying quiet of the interior desert of contemplative prayer. I'm not saying that contemplative prayer will heal legitimate mental illness. No, many of us would do well to cooperate with appropriate modern medicine. But while meds are intended to balance out our psychosis, a humble practice of contemplative prayer, with its roots in the fourth century desert mothers and fathers, has proven to still the tempest of my soul.

In *The Palace of Nowhere* James Finley writes, **"The desert where prayer flourishes is the desert of our own hearts barren of all the slogans that we have been led to believe to be our very identity and salvation. Prayer is a death to every identity that does not come from God."[68]**

For as long as I can remember I've battled with my sense of identity.

Who the hell am I, really?

Certain habits of prayer only seem to perpetuate my image-maintenance projects, those embarrassing desires to feel superior and on top. Centering prayer, the practice of a detoxifying, wordless pursuit of an interior desert, has seemed to further mold my heart in the shape of a humble acceptance of who I am, yielding a generous hospitality toward folks like Randy.

I'm slowly learning to love the desert.

A few years back a good friend introduced me to his favorite camping spot in an obscure piece of Utah desert. Among the rocks, lizards, and canyon birds is a quiet that's deeply and disturbingly quiet. It's a rare place, mostly devoid of human contact and cell phone reception. I quickly learned that even though you can travel out of the city to find exterior quiet, the interior quiet isn't nearly as easy to achieve.

If you're not accustomed to dwelling in an exterior quiet that confronts you with your own interior drama, silence can be one of the most challenging languages to learn. In his book *Contemplative Prayer*, Thomas Merton quotes St. Isaac the Syrian, a seventh-century hermit monk: "If you love truth, be a lover of silence. Silence, like the sunlight, will illuminate you in God."[69]

Loving silence is a practice and a deeply meaningful pursuit. Creative silence is a

necessary part of prayer. Pascal once said, "All the unhappiness of men arises from one single fact, that they cannot stay quietly in their own chamber."[70]

I've found this to be an enduring truth in my own life, and a frighteningly accurate reflection of the world we inhabit today. I hope to show my own boys, and all those they journey with, a different way.

When Josiah, our first child, was a newborn, I had to learn that just because he hadn't yet acquired advanced English didn't mean that we couldn't communicate with each other. In fact, if you want to be in relationship with newborns, elderly people on their death bed, your pets, or the deaf and mute, you'll be invited to appreciate the language of silence. When God spoke the world into existence, it wasn't necessarily audible. Silence is a language every bit as powerful as the spoken word.

Silence is God's native tongue.

After the creation of our planet, how many years went by before the music of subwoofers, honking horns, barking seals, or bouncing basketballs took over?

The Living Presence is a relationship born of consensual loving silence.

This consensual loving silence was modeled for me as I watched my wife sit in compassionate quiet with her mother as she was concluding her long journey with Alzheimer's. The look on Angela's face revealed that what they shared in these non-verbal moments was just as profound as any conversation they may have had twenty years ago.

It's in the silence that we turn our ear toward the voice of love.

Chances are that this may not have been the first thing you heard as you were learning to pray. For most of us, it takes many years to hear beyond the inner critic that calls us worthless, not to mention all the self-imposed judgments that have filled the basement of our heart with shame. It takes time and a relentless determination to move through the detoxifying process of silence and grief until we begin to hear and trust that healing voice.

Historically, the word we've used for turning one's ear toward love is the word "obedience." If you grew up with an image of God who was moody, stern-faced, and wouldn't let you wear your baseball cap in church, you probably have a dicey relationship with the word obedience. That abusive image of God has caused so many "ex-vangelicals" to avoid the practice of prayer altogether.

The root of obedience is the Latin verb *audere*, which means "to listen toward."[72] **In reality, obedience is the practice of listening toward the heart of reality, which is listening to the loving heart of God.**

I completely understand if the word "obedience" is too triggering to use today, but in its essence, obedient prayer is a divine listening posture which transcends the reactivity of fight or flight. Although I've had my share of rage-filled prayers (and those certainly have their place), obedient prayer is neither unhinged rage nor careless apathy. The ultimate image of obedient prayer is the disciple John, who faithfully rests his head on God's chest to listen for the divine heartbeat.

Words are a gift, but silence seems to be the most conducive space for this tender way of heart-to-heart connectivity.

But like any good thing (exercise, scotch, or sex to name a few), silence can be an idol—in its simplest form, an unhealthy attachment.

After preaching an Easter sermon which followed a particularly hard couple of months, I booked forty-eight hours at Sacred Heart, a silent retreat center just south of the Denver metro area. I had been anticipating this opportunity for some restful quiet for a long time.

Mornings at the retreat center are my favorite. I wake up early, get that first cup of coffee, and set up shop seated at a table in the fire-side room. My books, journal, coffee, and I watch the dawn light slowly tumble through stained-glass windows. On the first morning of this particular visit, I was slightly bummed to discover that I was the second one to arrive in the fire-side room. I had hoped to be alone in complete quiet, but my attitude was forgiving . . . until the paper shuffling began.

The man on the other side of the large room sounded as if he were meticulously tearing pieces of paper apart and then shaking them. Vigorously. What was he thinking? This IS a SILENT retreat center.

Surely, this won't last long, I thought.

No such luck. I spent several minutes staring coldly at him hoping his eyes would meet mine and realize the ridiculous disturbance he was creating. It didn't work. Is this a hidden camera gag? No cameras to be found. My simmer of initial curiosity slowly turned into a rolling boil. This was my time for rest, to re-center, to meet with God. And here's this joker sabotaging it all before the sun is fully up!

Agitated and resentful, I stood up, grabbed my materials, and strode out the door to go for a walk.

The next morning I set my alarm for 4:30 a.m. hoping to beat the mysterious paper-shuffling gangster. Mission accomplished. With a cup of fresh coffee in hand, I let out a deep exhale, and once again opened my journal to wade into deeper waters.

Ahhh, the ideal beginning of a restful day. Eventually, I became immersed in the book I was reading, energetically taking notes and then . . . damn it! Here we go again. That crinkling paper across the room began taunting me like a cocky rooster.

Once again, I relented and headed back to my room—this time with more curiosity than anger. This was my last morning at the retreat center before heading back to the city, and I began wondering what the Spirit was really trying to teach me.

As I was leaving later that day, I looked down the long hall and there he was, the paper gangster sitting in a chair quietly reading. I determined it was time to put that obedient prayer thing into practice and listen *toward* him. I walked down the hall and introduced myself with a smile, breaking the rules of silence as I said: "I've noticed you've been working on a project while I've been here. Mind if I ask what it is you're up to?"

His weathered and pain-filled face looked up at me as he handed me his tattered Bible. "This was my mother's Bible," he said. "Last year, her and I was caught in a flood. Washed our car clean off the road and into the river. Tried to save my mom but the current swept her away. But as I struggled for my own life, I was able to salvage her Bible. It's all I got left of her."

I was shocked and sobered as I listened. He continued, "As I was drying it out, the pages stuck together, so I spent the past two days pulling all the pages apart. I'm almost finished."

Sometimes this is what it looks like to lay our head on God's chest and listen to the heartbeat of Christ.

The gangster I so terribly resented, like all gangsters, had a traumatic backstory. As he noisily restored those fragile pages, he intimately interacted with memories of his mother. His actions, perhaps inconsiderate at a silent retreat center, were a legitimate, determined practice of grief. It occurred to me that it's true what they say—grief looks (and sounds) different from person to person.

On the silent drive home, I realized how I had idealized, if not idolized, the practice of quiet. I'm still not sure why he chose a silent retreat center to do this work, but once my heart awakened and shifted from my one-sided assumptions, not only did my frustration dissolve, but I stumbled on a powerful personal illustration for prayer. Those crinkled pages are forever stuck in mind.

Silence is a way to connect with God, but it's not the only way. It's a needed gift, but if I *need* it like the alcoholic needs his next drink, or in a way that creates resentment and blame, then the gift becomes just another unhealthy attachment. Most of my friends who sleep in alleyways and on steam grates cannot afford this gift of exterior silence. The poor around the globe dwelling in urban slums or dilapidated trailer parks have no concept of the privilege of heading off to camp in the desert or to rest at a quiet retreat center.

Idolatry is a one-sided conversation. It's the temptation the Israelites fell into along their wilderness journey. After being immersed in the Egyptian empire where expectations and outcomes were clear, their consciousness was not ready for the language of mystery, paradox, and silence. So, they figured out a way that they could do all the talking; they got busy molding a golden calf.[72]

But we're more advanced than those primitive, idolatrous Hebrews, right? Hold up, let me send this tweet out, respond to these emails, finish chapter seven, schedule that meeting, and get the boys to baseball practice.

Decades before the phenomenon of social media, Thomas Merton speaks of superficial exterior appearances. Superficial. Exterior. Appearances. These are the distracting apparitions which tend to form our routine visions of the world and the self. They are as ancient as any golden cow and can come in almost any shape or form.

We're all prone to preoccupation, impatience, and choosing golden cows over the Real Thing. While catching my preoccupations in the act is helpful, the practice of contemplative prayer is a gesture of welcoming and resting in the Living Presence. Thomas Merton describes contemplative silence as a gesture of consent.

"When I consent to the will and the mercy of God as it 'comes' to me in the events of life, appealing to my inner self and awakening my faith, I break through the superficial exterior appearances that form my routine vision of the world and of my own self, and I find myself in the presence of hidden majesty."[73]

In light of this primal temptation, the Psalmist says, "For God alone my soul waits in silence . . ."[74]

When Randy or any of us find ourselves caught in the frantic bipolar reactivity of fight or flight, it's intentional silent waiting that allows us to lend our ear toward the heart of the Living Presence. In the Hebrew scriptures, the verb meaning to wait is the word *qavah*, which is defined as "a binding together." It's similar to the Latin roots of our word for religion, which is also defined as "a binding together."[75]

For me, the practice of contemplative prayer has indeed become the tie that binds. It's how we soften our heart like putty, how we consent to the work of silence and truly listen, and how we once again hear the rhythm of the divine heartbeat. May we all open up to this invitation to re-connect with the Living Presence in a radically different way. Prayer and putty.

The quality of one's life depends on the quality of attention. Whatever you pay attention to will grow more important in your life.

—Deepok Chopra

THE SOUND
BELCHES & BURNING BUSHES

"Hey dad, listen to the way Micah's belch echoes off that house!"

There are several meaningful words of depth strewn throughout these pages, but it's phrases like these which spill out of my home every day that I treasure most.

If I can't find the space for a belching contest with my eleven and nine-year-old sons during a Sunday evening stroll through the neighborhood, then I'm not really participating with the irrelevant Christ. Didn't the author of Ecclesiastes say that there is a time and purpose for everything? Sorry, neighbors!

Shortly after that awful belching ensemble by the Taylor trio, I invited the boys into five minutes of silence as we walk. And that's the culture of our home in a nutshell—testing the limits of bodily noises in one moment, quiet prayer in the next. They know this routine as one of the rhythms of our life.

After setting a timer for five minutes, we deliberately slow down our pace and listen to the sounds that surround us, as well as the sound of our own heartbeats and desires.

As we quietly walk in the fading glow of daylight, everything seems a little more subdued. Micah pauses, turns to face a particular tree, and then meticulously observes its leaves. Then he whispers, "Dad what kind of tree is this?" It is a young, unimpressive maple tree, but apparently, something about it had called out to Micah. He pulls off a leaf, gently and reverently holds and examines it, and then continues walking with leaf in hand.

On our way back home, we cross the interstate overpass and again Micah pauses, this time to quietly observe the traffic coming and going beneath him. He extends the leaf out in front of him with his right hand as his gaze subtly shifts back and forth between the traffic and the leaf. The whole scene—near and far—is deserving of his careful attention.

I feel a mixture of awe and a tickle of humor rise in me. An hour earlier that same kid was bouncing his belches off of houses while his brother and I rated them like Olympic judges. And now, in this particular moment, he's completely consumed in some type of spiritual encounter.

What in the world was transpiring within this young man in that moment? I stood there, about forty yards away from Micah, paying attention to him paying attention to that leaf and the passing traffic. As I observed him, my own perception of time seemed to unconsciously drift into some other dimension. How long had we been standing there—five minutes or thirty seconds?

This is the Christ Mystery.

There are moments when a belching contest with pre-adolescent boys makes perfect sense, and there are moments when all of infinity seems to graciously collapse into the present moment. Any distinction between the two is illusion.

So, we pay attention. We slow down enough to curiously consider what's really going on.

This is the mysticism hidden within ordinary experience. Like an everyday burning bush. In fact, let's revisit the ancient story of Moses from Exodus chapter three.

And the angel of the Lord appeared unto him in a flame of fire out of the midst of a bush: and he looked, and, behold, the bush burned with fire, and the bush was not consumed.

And Moses said, "I will now turn aside, and see this great sight, why the bush is not burnt."

And when the Lord saw that he turned aside to see, God called unto him out of the midst of the bush, and said, "Moses, Moses."

And he said, "Here am I."[76]

In this timeless story, we find ourselves caught up in a bizarre sci-fi scene of a blazing shrub that talks, but let's pause to consider what's really going on. What do you suppose the author is truly attempting to emphasize? Twice, our attention is called to the phrase "turn aside."

Like Micah with his maple leaf, something was calling out to Moses, so he followed his heart to fully notice it. In this moment, the Living Presence noticed that Moses was noticing. And in that moment, Moses heard the sound of God's voice. Moses then paused and examined the scene with the eyes of his heart.

God is that parent observing us as we walk, noticing us as we notice the maple leaf. He notices us as we reflect again on the sound of Steve Myer's laugh, or the simple beauty of the mourning dove, or the heart's desperate cry beneath a friend's disturbing rage.

If I haven't conveyed it clearly enough, allow me to spell it out now. This is a book about noticing the divine depths within our everyday experiences. We all have the capacity to notice. You don't have to live in a monastery or possess a seminary degree. You don't even have to live indoors to reverently and gently hold the following questions:

» Can I see Christ in the seemingly irrelevant stuff of life?

» Am I willing to develop the practices to do so?

» Can this way of seeing become memorized within the rhythmic muscle at my core—the very one through which life flows in and out?

I know these are traditionally the type of questions a monk, philosopher, or a good theologian or scientist might ask, but God didn't intend for humans to identify with those labels more than the basic "human" one we all share.

We all have access to this contemplative vision of the world and in my observation, children, along with the poor, may be some of our most powerful and overlooked mystics. At first glance you wouldn't describe my occasionally goofy nine-year-old or my imprisoned friend

Vinny as a mystic, but they are. And that's the point.

Hagar, a slave of Abram, was another overlooked mystic. After Hagar conceived Abram's first son (at the couple's demand), his jealous wife Sarai kicks her out into the wilderness. Now a publicly shamed, abandoned, homeless single mom, Hagar has an encounter with the Living Presence that she describes like this: "You are the God who sees me . . . I have now seen the One who sees me."[77]

Perceived as no more than a discarded piece of property, God notices Hagar. And God notices you. And God invites you to see yourself in the reflection of divine eyes, just like he did with Hagar. Believing that we are seen and known nourishes the heart like nothing else; it allows us to become humble people.

Throughout history, the poor, the simple, and the suffering seem to be among those who are humble enough to notice the One who notices them. It's always the humble ones who seem to encounter God in the pain and monotony of everyday life.

Mystics are not people who are more intelligent or holy than others, and they aren't always articulate or well-behaved. Mystics are simply those who humbly practice *turning aside* as a way of life. Mystics are those who gaze in reverent

126

wonder at the things everyone else seems to overlook. They're not eccentrics who have disciplined habits of fasting, who seldom bathe, or who sit quietly for hours in the lotus position. The mystic is about the mutual healing and wholeness that comes when we pay attention to the Living Presence in all things.

The mystic is also one who respects the varied contours of space and time.

The ancient Greeks had two different words for the concept of time—*chronos* and *kairos.* The word *chronos* refers to our day-to-day measurement of the ticktocks. We wear watches on our wrist and hang clocks on our walls because this form of time focuses us on duration and allows most of us to pay the bills. But, when we allow this form of time to dictate, dominate, and direct our lives, we can be sure that it will never transform our hearts.

The "other" form of time—the irrelevant form of time—is called *kairos.* Philosophers and mystics refer to this as "deep time." When Moses turned aside, there was a mysterious undercurrent that propelled him to transition from chronological to "kairological" time.

Writing this book has served me in a similar way. As I tinkered with these chapters over the years, there have undoubtedly been plenty of humdrum *chronos* moments when I wanted nothing more than to push the hands of time along and get this project over with. To be honest though, as a whole, this practice of reflection and writing about my relationships, awkward experiences, and significant learnings has re-awakened me to a more generative perspective of deep time.

Now, as the pastor of a small urban ministry to the unhoused and detached, so many of my days are filled with the obligatory unclogging of toilets, paying of bills, communication of clear boundaries, and breathing through anxiety over the budget. The practice of organizing these words, however, has afforded me the privilege of stepping back several paces to notice what I've turned aside to notice over the years.

As I've turned aside, I've been able to take a more panoramic snapshot of my ever-unfolding spiritual journey. I've connected dots that previously didn't add up and even created more meaning out of challenging seasons of depression, deep loneliness, and so many circumstances in which I had internalized the awkwardness as shame. The contemplative work of writing has played a surprising role in allowing my eyes to adjust to the reality of *kairos*.

One thing I can say with assurance is that translating experiences with the divine—from *kairos* to *chronos* to words on a page—can be clunky, frustrating, painful, humbling, and breathtakingly beautiful. There are more metaphors in these pages than I care to count, but they're how we experience and communicate God—to ourselves and to others. They're how God reveals Godself to us when we pause, notice, listen, and know that we're deeply seen and intimately known.

I didn't know *kairos* from a basketball as a young adult. And I can't say that I've been particularly elegant or eloquent as I've made my way to whoever I am now, but I have tried to faithfully relay in my writing some of the breadth and depth that I've been given. And I can say whole-heartedly that the snapshots, fragments, and anecdotes of people and experiences in these pages have been some of my best teachers: Steve Myer and Jenga, Miss Oneta and the waterlines, a bird on a wire, a lone cloud, a red-sweater protest followed by crying in my breakfast, a grieving son at a silent retreat center, and a boy and his maple leaf.

As I wind down this last chapter, I'm compelled to zero in on a clear message that I hope you'll take seriously. It's really not that complicated. It goes like this:

» Release your expectations.

» Return to your holy desire.

» Trust yourself as you sink into the reality

that even now, in this very moment, God notices you.

The path toward this expanded way of seeing the world comes with the divine invitation to release those narrow outcomes that have triggered your migraines, accusations, and angry outbursts over the years. Those expectations didn't start out as toxic. At one time, they were unique, holy yearnings stemming from the depths of your one wild and precious life.

I know you've wrestled with this message throughout your life as well. For me, writing this book has felt a bit like a culmination of decades of writhing and wrestling with questions about who I am, the nature of God, and whether I can truly trust the depths of me.

We have been given permission to become intimately acquainted with our own experiences, and intimacy is always preceded by great trust. **Deep trust is the antidote to the illusion of separateness.** The reality is you can never be separated from the Cosmic Christ except for in your own mind. This is why Jesus and Paul so clearly invited us into a new consciousness—a new mind where we are invited to see abundance rather than scarcity.

When we are living in Christ, we recognize that we have been infinitely befriended by a Living Presence who excludes no one. This awareness

takes us by the hand and leads us into a vision of expansion rather than limitation. It re-aligns our perspective from the confines of chronological time to the wide-reaching possibilities of *kairos.*

If you're still reading, I trust that you know the truth—that you are being led. The Living Presence is drawing you further on and deeper down.

The intricacies of the maple leaf are offering us clues to the cosmos. When we lean in and attentively listen, we hear the whispers of resurrection. The voice is a sound that connects us with Harriet Tubman, Henri Nouwen, Moses, and even Jesus himself.

We can trust that our wounds, confusions, and unique personal hiccups are each magically laced with the energy of resurrection. Remember, God comes to us disguised as our life.

Your life is so much larger than the constricted confines of status quo comforts and security within the cul-de-sac of a precious little nuclear family. If you're feeling the invitation to take a risk, live with greater intention, and follow Christ below the waterline, then take that step with assurance. Understand that deep down you are seen, held, and known within the Big Mystery.

You know there's a larger, more diverse framework—a cosmic imagination just waiting to be birthed within you. Its power is subversive, like the sound of a flute echoing off canyon walls. Its presence resides among seemingly irrelevant people and places. And its timing is unimaginably mysterious.

Let yourself be drawn further on and deeper down. Listen.

In the beginning was the sound.

Can you hear it?

Want to help support the work of long-term redemptive relationships at Network Coffee House? Please visit **networkcoffeehouse.org** to learn more.

You can also follow Network on Facebook & Instagram **@networkcoffeehouse**.

Want Ryan to come speak at your church or gathering? Email **ryan@networkcoffeehouse.org** or call **303-830-1508**.

A BENEDICTION

At the beginning of chapter three, I made mention of an angry neighbor who broke one of our windows and shouted all kinds of venom toward our community. After he finally walked away, I invited everyone inside the coffeehouse for a needed family talk. In that moment of intensity, hurt, and disorientation we developed the following litany which has become the benediction for Urban Mercy church and a re-membering mantra for Network.

It's not all that complex. Please feel welcome to pause, breathe, and receive these words for yourself as well as use them in your communities.

We are made in God's image.
We are made of love not shame.
We are never alone.
Christ is with us.
Do not be afraid.

ACKNOWLEDGMENTS

A large cup of gratitude goes to . . .

Angela, twenty years in. We're still here and yet it feels like we're just getting started.

All my friends, staff, and volunteers around Network, Urban Mercy, and the larger network of fellow sojourners walking alongside me. The story somehow keeps getting written. We'll just be attentive and participate.

To elder influences Jeff Johnsen, Penny Salazar, Scott Dewey, Scott Jenkins, and all the fine folks of Mile High Ministries.

To my good friend and mentor, the late John Hicks.

To Rabbi Alan Ullman, Rabbi Nahum Ward-Lev, Wes Roberts, and my therapist Ellen.

Special thanks to Richard Rohr and all the wonderful teachers within The Living School for Action and Contemplation.

I'm grateful for old school hip-hop and the '90s alt rock tunes that provide my life soundtrack. And during the last season of this book, I'm grateful for NF and U2 who kept my feet moving.

And lastly. Thank you Josiah and Micah, along with Freddy the Dog, for letting me be your dad.

A BIBLIOGRAPHY

EPIGRAPHS

Moltmann, Jürgen. "The mysticism of everyday life..." in *Seven Sacred Pauses: Living Mindfully through the Hours of the Day* by Wiederkehr, Macrina, and Paula D'Arcy. 2008. Notre Dame, IN: Sorin Books.

[Chapter 1] Nouwen, Henri J. M. 1989. *In The Name of Jesus.* New York: Crossroad.

[Chapter 2] Barks, Coleman. 1996. *The Essential Rumi.* New York: Harper San Francisco.

[Chapter 3] Jay-Z. 2011. *Decoded.* New York: Spiegel & Grau.

[Chapter 4] King, Martin Luther. *A Testament of Hope: the Essential Writings of Martin Luther King, Jr.* Edited by James Melvin. (1986) 1991. Washington. New York: Harper San Francisco.

[Chapter 5] D'Arcy, Paula. "God comes to us disguised as our life," in *Everything Belongs: the Gift of Contemplative Prayer* by Richard Rohr. (1999) 2003. New York: The Crossroad Publishing Company.

[Chapter 6] Finley, James. "Opening Session." Speech, Living School Symposium, Center for Action and Contemplation. Albuquerque, NM: August 6, 2018.

[Chapter 7] Pascal, Blaise. 1660. *Pensées.* Translated by W. F. Trotter. http://www.leaderu.com /cyber/books/pensees/ pensees-SECTION-2.html

[Chapter 8] Chopra, Deepak. 2010. *Ageless Body, Timeless Mind: the Quantum Alternative to Growing Old.* New York: Three Rivers Press.

WORKS CONSULTED

Aland, Kurt, Matthew Black, Bruce M. Metzger, and Allen Wikgren, eds. (1966) 2001. *The Greek New Testament.* Stuttgard, Germany: Deutsche Bibelgesellschaft.

Mounce, William D. 1993. *The Analytical Lexicon to the Greek New Testament.* Grand Rapids, Michigan: Zondervan.

Notes from lectures during my time studying at the Living School (2016–2018), a part of the Center for Action and Contemplation, under the tutelage of Dr. James Finley, Fr. Richard Rohr, and Rev. Cynthia Bourgeault among others.

Notes on Hebrew and Latin text from various conversations and Scripture Circles with Rabbi Alan Ulman and his son Noah. Scripture Circles are a way of studying the Scriptures that is practical and pastoral, scholarly and mystical, personal and communal.

WORKS CITED

Bourgeault, Cynthia. 2008. *The Wisdom of Jesus: Transforming Heart and Mind: a New Perspective on Christ and His Message.* Boston & London: Shambhala.

Boyle, Gregory. "The Power of Boundless Compassion." Speech, Colorado Springs, CO. October 4, 2018.

Cragg, Kenneth. (1976) 2009. *The Wisdom of the Sufis.* Mount

Jackson, VA: Axios Press.

"Christa McAuliffe Biography." Biography.com. A&E Networks Television. Updated July 23, 2019. https://www.biography.com/astronaut/christa-mcauliffe.

de Chardin, Pierre Teilhard. 1965. *The Divine Milieu*. New York: Harper & Row.

———. 1975. *On Suffering*. London: Collins.

Favreu, John, dir. *Elf*. 2003. Los Angeles, California: New Line Cinema, DVD.

Finley, James. "The Contemplative Mind of Christ." Speech, Living School Symposium, Center for Action and Contemplation. Albuquerque, NM: August, 2016.

———. *Merton's Palace of Nowhere*. 2018. Notre Dame, IN: Ave Maria Press.

Isaac the Syrian, Saint. "If you love truth..." in *Contemplative Prayer* by Thomas Merton. (1969) 1996. New York: Image Books.

Kidd, Sue Monk. (1990) 2006. *When the Heart Waits*. New York: HarperOne.

Knuth, Jane. 2010. *The Thrift Store Saints: Meeting Jesus 25¢ at a Time*. Chicago, Illinois: Loyola Press.

Merton, Thomas. 1965. *Conjectures of a Guilty Bystander*. New York: Image Books.

———. (1961) 2007. *New Seeds of Contemplation*. New York: New Directions.

———. "My life is measured..." in *Run to the Mountain: The Journals of Thomas Merton Volume One 1939:-1941*. Edited by Patrick Hart. 1996. New York: HarperCollins.

Network Coffee House. Accessed May 28, 2020. https://networkcoffeehouse.org/.

Nouwen, Henri J. M. (1974) 2004. *Out of Solitude: Three Meditations on the Christian Life*. Notre Dame, IN: Ave Maria Press.

O'Donohue, John. 1998. *Anam Cara: A Book of Celtic Wisdom*. New York: Perennial.

Oliver, Mary. 2017. *Devotions: The Selected Poems of Mary Oliver*. New York: Penguin Press.

———. 2006. *New and Selected Poems. Vol. 2*. Boston, MA: Beacon.

Rohr, Richard. 2018. *Essential Teachings on Love*. Maryknoll, NY: Orbis Books.

———. 2019. *The Universal Christ: How a Forgotten Reality Can Change Everything We See, Hope for, and Believe*. New York: Convergent Books.

Sanford, John Arthur. 1989. *Dreams: Gods Forgotten Language*. San Francisco, CA: Harper & Row.

Teresa, of Ávila Saint. 2008. *The Interior Castle*. Alachua,

Florida: Bridge-Logos.

Thích Nhất Hạnh, "We are here to awaken…" in "7 Zen Teachings from to Live By" by Sofia Marbach. *Pachamama Alliance* (blog). April 7, 2016. https://blog. pachamama.org / 7-zen-teachings-from-thich-nhat-hanh-to-live-by.

Thurman, Howard. (1953) 1999. *Meditations of the Heart.* Boston, MA: Beacon Press.

"40," U2, Spotify, track 10 on War, Island Records, 1983.

NOTES

Chapter 1
1. Cragg, *The Wisdom of the Sufis*, 49.
2. Nouwen, *In the Name of Jesus*, 17.
3. Barney Fife, played by Don Knotts, was the main character in *The Andy Griffith Show* that aired from 1960-1968.
4. Knuth, *The Thrift Store Saints: Meeting Jesus 25¢ at a Time*, xi.

Chapter 2
5. Isaiah 30:15 (TLB)
6. Network Coffee House, accessed May 28, 2020, https:// networkcoffeehouse.org/.
7. Merton, in *Run to the Mountain, 399.*
8. Luke 5:4 (NLT)
9. Bourgeault, *The Wisdom of Jesus,* 44.
10. Genesis 37:5-9 (NLT)
11. Genesis 12-25
12. Numbers 14:30-34, Joshua 5:6
13. Matthew 4:1-11

14. "40," U2, Spotify, track 10 on War, Island Records, 1983.
15. "40," U2 Vertigo Tour, Denver, Colorado, April 20, 2005. "40" was the last song of the encore performance.
16. Genesis 7:12
17. Exodus 24:18
18. Deuteronomy 8:2-5
19. Matthew 4:1-11
20. Acts 1:4
21. Jonah 1:17-2:10
22. de Chardin, *On Suffering*, 84.
23. John 3:3 (NIV)
24. John 3:1-15
25. Kidd, *When the Heart Waits*, 48.

Chapter 3
26. Notes from Scripture Circles with Rabbi Ullman.
27. Matthew 17
28. Merton, *Conjectures of a Guilty Bystander*, 153–154.
29. Teresa, of Ávila,*The Interior Castle*, 30. Saint Teresa was a Spanish Carmelite nun and famed mystic who wrote The Interior Castle in 1577 as a guide for spiritual development through service and prayer.
30. Rohr, *The Universal Christ*, 52.
31. Oliver, *New and Selected Poems Volume 2*, 104.
32. de Chardin, *The Divine Milieu*, 86.
33. John 20:11-18
34. Luke 24:13-35
35. Numbers 22
36. Exodus 3
37. Psalm 42:7 (NIV)
38. Philippians 2:7

Chapter 4
39. John 15:15 (NIV)
40. The Omega Point is a term coined by French Jesuit priest, Pierre Teilhard de Chardin, meaning everything

in the universe is fated to spiral towards a final point of unification.

41. Boyle, "The Power of Boundless Compassion," (speech, Colorado Springs, CO, October 4, 2018).

42. Thích Nhất Hạnh, "We are here to awaken..." in "7 Zen Teachings from to Live By" by Sofia Marbach. *Pachamama Alliance* (blog).

43. Nouwen, *Out of Solitude*, 38.

44. *Kola* is the Lakota word for "friend."

45. Hebrews 13:13 (NIV)

46. Isaiah 41:8 (NLT, my italics).

47. 2 Chronicles 20:7 (NLT, my italics).

48. Notes on Hebrew translations from Scripture Circles with Rabbi Ullman.

49. Genesis 22:1-19

50. O'Donohue, *Anam Cara*, 14.

51. A circle dance is a *perrichoresis*, which describes the relational movement found in the very heart of trinitarian spirituality.

52. de Chardin, *The Divine Milieu*, 139.

Chapter 5

53. "Christa McAuliffe Biography," Updated July 23, 2019. Biography.com, https://www.biography .com/ astronaut/christa-mcauliffe

54. Matthew 22:36-39 (NIV)

55. Mounce, *The Analytical Lexicon to the Greek New Testament*.

56. By non-binary awareness, I mean a way of processing reality that is able to transcend black-and-white and either/or thinking. While that way of thinking is imperative in our youth, reality becomes much grayer as we grow older, and we must employ more both/and thinking.

57. John 20:11-18

58. Luke 24:13-32
59. Current events in Jerusalem included Jesus having been betrayed by Judas, arrested, flogged, crucified, mocked, hung on the cross to die, and later entombed. (John 13-19)
60. Oliver, *Devotions*, 316.
61. Finley, "The Contemplative Mind of Christ" (lecture, Albuquerque, New Mexico, August 2016).
62. Sanford, *Dreams: Gods Forgotten Language*, xii.
63. Rohr, *Essential Teachings on Love*.

Chapter 6

64. Buddy the Elf is a character played by Will Ferrell in the movie *Elf*. 2003.
65. Finley, "The Contemplative Mind of Christ" (lecture, Albuquerque, NM: August, 2016).
66. Matthew 26:6-13, Mark 14:3-9, Luke 7:36-50, John 12:2-7
67. Thurman, *Meditations of the Heart*, 174-175.

Chapter 7

68. Finley, *Merton's Palace of Nowhere*, 51.
69. St. Isaac in *Contemplative Prayer*, 5.
70. Pascal, *Pensées*, Section II, *Pensée* 139.
    Blaise Pascal was a French mathematician, physicist, inventor, writer and Catholic theologian who lived from 1623–1662.
71. Notes from Scripture Circles with Rabbi Ullman
72. Exodus 32
73. Merton, *New Seeds of Contemplation*, 41.
74. Psalm 62:1 (ESV)

Chapter 8

75. Notes on Hebrew and Latin translations from Scripture Circles with Rabbi Ullman.
76. Exodus 3:2-4 (KJV). The "turn aside" translation can be found in the King James interpretation, which in this instance, is much closer to the original Hebrew.

77. Genesis 16:13 (NIV)